REVISE PEARSON EDEXCEL GCSE (9–1)
Mathematics
FOUNDATION
BOOTCAMP

Series consultant: Harry Smith
Author: Harry Smith

Also available to support your revision:

Revise GCSE Study Skills Guide   9781447967071

The **Revise GCSE Study Skills Guide** is full of tried-and-trusted hints and tips for how to learn more effectively. It gives you techniques to help you achieve your best – throughout your GCSE studies and beyond?

Revise GCSE Revision Planner   9781447967828

The **Revise GCSE Revision Planner** helps you to plan and organise your time, step-by-step, throughout your GCSE revision. Use this book and wall chart to mastermind your revision

For the full range of Pearson revision titles across KS2, KS3, GCSE, Functional Skills, AS/A Level and BTEC visit:
www.pearsonschools.co.uk/revise

Welcome to Bootcamp

GCSE Maths Bootcamp is designed to help you squeeze the maximum amount of useful revision into the minimum amount of time. This book contains 30 short workouts, which can each be completed in about 20 minutes. Finish the whole book and you can be exam-fit in just 10 hours!

Check out these great features that appear on each workout.

Quick warm-ups remind you of the key facts and formulae for this workout.

Use this tracker to check your progress at-a-glance. This is Workout 11, so you are nearly half-way there!

Exam-standard questions so you can be confident you're revising at the right level.

If you need a bit more help, check out these pages in the *Pearson Edexcel GCSE Maths Foundation Revision Guide*.

Super strategies to help you master problem-solving questions.

Get the inside track with these top exam tips from our experts.

Build your confidence with these reps. The first one has been done for you each time.

Tick off each workout once you have finished it.

The scale next to each question tells you how difficult it is. If you are stuck on a tricky question, try coming back to it later.

Guided We've given you a head start on some questions. Look out for this "guided" icon and complete the working to find the correct solution.

Contents

1. Number crunch
2. Fractions and decimals
3. Powers and roots
4. Rounding, estimation and error
5. Factors, multiples and primes
6. Algebra essentials
7. Brackets and factorising
8. Equations and inequalities
9. Formulae
10. Sequences
11. Coordinates and lines
12. Real-life graphs
13. Curvy graphs
14. Tricky algebra
15. Percentages
16. Ratio and proportion
17. Measuring and estimating
18. Compound measures
19. All the angles
20. Perimeter and area
21. 3-D shapes
22. Circles and cylinders
23. Transformations
24. Pythagoras and trigonometry
25. Bearings and constructions
26. Similar and congruent
27. Graphs and charts
28. Averages and range
29. Probability
30. Venn diagrams

Answers

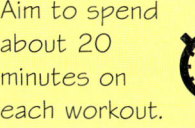

Aim to spend about 20 minutes on each workout.

You will find answers to the reps questions and full worked solutions to all the exam-style questions at the back of the book. Use them to check your progress.

1 Number crunch

Warm up

✓ The position of each digit in a number tells you its value.

Thousands | Hundreds | Tens | Units . Tenths | Hundredths
7 5 0 1
     3 . 4 7

✓ You can order negative numbers using a number line.

← NEGATIVE NUMBERS | POSITIVE NUMBERS →
−5 −4 −3 −2 −1 0 1 2 3 4 5

✓ Negative × Negative = Positive

✓ Positive × Negative = Negative

✓ Negative × Positive = Negative

✓ You need to be able to **add**, **subtract**, **multiply** and **divide** numbers using mental and written methods.

```
   1 7 4          ⁴5̶ ¹1 9          2 5 7              2 1 3
 + 2 8 2         −   3 2         ×     3          8 )1 7 ¹0 ²4
   ─────          ─────           ─────
   4 5 6           4 8 7           7 7 1
     ₁                              ₁ ₂
```

Reps

1 In the number 3215.49 write down the value of

the 3   **3 thousands**
a the 1   ....
b the 4   ....
c the 5   ....
d the 2   ....

2 Write in order, smallest first.

4   −1   2   **−1   2   4**
a 40   30   9   ....
b −3   −8   0   ....
c 5   −10   7   ....
d 21   −3   −5   ....

3 Work out mentally

−4 × −9   **36**
a −3 × 20   ....
b 30 × 8   ....
c 120 ÷ 4   ....
d 90 ÷ 6   ....

4 Use a written method to work out

23 × 15   **345**
a 137 × 21   ....
b 2275 − 188 ....
c 1617 ÷ 7   ....
d 452 + 1296 ....

GCSE Maths: Bootcamp

Exam practice

1. Here are four different digits.

   7   5   1   9

   (a) Write one digit in each box to give the sum with the largest possible answer. One has been done for you. You may only use each digit once.

   Guided

   (1 mark)

   > The operation is subtraction. This means the first 2-digit number needs to be as large as possible and the second 2-digit number needs to be as small as possible.

   (b) Use three of the digits above to make the smallest possible positive number. **(1 mark)**

   > Make sure you write a 3-digit number as your answer.

   ....

Problem solved!

2. Angela buys:
   - 6 exercise books costing £1.20 each
   - 1 pencil sharpener costing 80p
   - 3 ink cartridges.

   She pays with a £10 note and gets 65p change.
   Work out the cost of one ink cartridge.
   You must show all your working.

   (3 marks)

   > If you are solving a money problem, you should work in either pounds or pence, but not both.

   > Make sure you show all your working, and copy figures carefully from the question.

Top exam tip!

Learn your times tables up to 12 × 12. It will make lots of calculations easier in your exam.

2 Fractions and decimals

Warm up

✓ Tips for working with decimal numbers:

Add or subtract	Multiply	Divide
Line up the decimal points then use a column method	Ignore decimal points, then count the total number of decimal digits in the calculation and use this in your answer	Multiply both values by 10, 100 or 1000 to make the second number a whole number

✓ Tips for working with fractions:

Add or subtract	Multiply	Divide	Mixed numbers
Find equivalent fractions with the same denominator	Multiply the numerators and the denominators	Turn the second fraction upside down then multiply	Write as improper fractions first

Reps

1 Work out

$4.2 + 3.6$ 7.8

a) $12.7 + 9.2$ ....
b) $20.3 - 5.9$ ....
c) 3.2×6 ....
d) $12.5 \div 5$ ....

2 Fill in the equivalent fractions. $\frac{2}{3} = \frac{6}{9}$

a) $\frac{1}{5} = \frac{\square}{15}$
b) $\frac{\square}{4} = \frac{9}{12}$
c) $\frac{2}{5} = \frac{10}{\square}$
d) $\frac{15}{\square} = \frac{3}{4}$

3 Find

$\frac{1}{3}$ of 600 g   200 g

a) $\frac{1}{2}$ of 200 ml .... ml
b) $\frac{2}{3}$ of 90 km .... km
c) $\frac{3}{5}$ of 60 kg .... kg
d) $\frac{9}{10}$ of 5 cm .... cm

4 Work out

$\frac{1}{5} + \frac{1}{2}$ $\frac{7}{10}$

a) $\frac{1}{2} + \frac{1}{4}$ ....
b) $\frac{1}{2} \times \frac{3}{5}$ ....
c) $4\frac{2}{3} - 2\frac{1}{4}$ ....
d) $\frac{1}{6} \div \frac{3}{4}$ ....

GCSE Maths: Bootcamp

Exam practice

 1. Alice thinks of a number.

$\frac{1}{4}$ of Alice's number is 10

Work out $\frac{2}{5}$ of Alice's number. (2 marks)

> To find a fraction of an amount you divide by the denominator, then multiply by the numerator.

Guided
10 × 4 = ...

.... ÷ 5 = ...

.... × 2 = ...

 2. Work out 24.7 × 5.8 (3 marks)

Guided
```
    2 4 7
  ×   5 8
  ───────
        0
  ───────
```
2 decimal places

> Ignore the decimal points and work out 247 × 58 using long multiplication. There are 2 decimal digits altogether in the question, so make sure there are 2 decimal digits in the answer.

....

 3. Work out $1\frac{1}{4} \times 2\frac{3}{5}$

Give your answer as a mixed number. (3 marks)

> Convert both mixed numbers to improper fractions:
>
> $2\frac{3}{5} = \frac{2 \times 5 + 3}{5} = \frac{13}{5}$

Top exam tip!

Show each step of your working clearly. You might get some marks even if you get the wrong answer.

....

3 Powers and roots

Warm up

✓ Use **BIDMAS** to remember the order of operations:
  Brackets → Indices → Division → Multiplication → Addition → Subtraction

✓ Use the index laws to simplify powers:

  ① $a^m \times a^n = a^{m+n}$ ② $(a^m)^n = a^{mn}$ ③ $\dfrac{a^m}{a^n} = a^{m-n}$

  ④ $a^{-n} = \dfrac{1}{a^n}$ ⑤ $\left(\dfrac{a}{b}\right)^n = \dfrac{a^n}{b^n}$ ⑥ $a^{\frac{1}{n}} = \sqrt[n]{a}$

✓ $a^1 = a$ and $a^0 = 1$ for any number a.

✓ Numbers in **standard form** are written in two parts:

$$2.6 \times 10^9$$

A number part that is greater than or equal to 1 and less than 10 ← → An integer power of 10

Reps

1 Work out

  9^2 81

a 11^2 ....
b $(3+1)^0$ ....
c $\sqrt{225}$ ....
d $5^2 - 2 \times 4$ ....

2 Write as a single power of 5

  $5^3 \times 5$ 5^4

a $5^2 \times 5^7$ ....
b $(5^3)^2$ ....
c $\dfrac{1}{125}$ ....
d 25^5 ....

3 Write in standard form

  0.0035 3.5×10^{-3}

a 29 000   ....
b 0.05   ....
c 9 010 000   ....
d 0.000 06   ....

4 Write as an ordinary number

  1.8×10^5 180 000

a 6.9×10^{-1} ....
b 8×10^4 ....
c 2.03×10^2 ....
d 5.5×10^{-3} ....

GCSE Maths: Bootcamp

Exam practice

1. Work out the value of
(a) $(7.1 - 2.5)^2 - 4.35$ **(2 marks)**

Guided

$7.1 - 2.5 = \ldots\ldots\ldots$
$\ldots\ldots^2 = \ldots\ldots$
$\ldots\ldots - 4.35 = \ldots\ldots$

(b) 3^{-2} **(1 mark)**

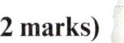 **Links to:** Pages 8, 9, 17, 18

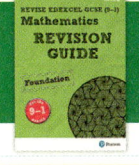

Write down your working even when you are using a calculator. Work out the brackets first, then square this result before subtracting 4.35.

....

2. Work out $(6.5 \times 10^8) \times (2 \times 10^{-13})$
Give your answer as an ordinary number. **(2 marks)**

You can enter numbers in standard form into your calculator using the $\boxed{\times 10^x}$ key.

....

3. Work out $\dfrac{0.05 \times 0.0007}{0.01}$

Give your answer in standard form. **(3 marks)**

You can multiply numbers in standard form without a calculator by multiplying the number parts then adding the powers of 10. Dividing by 0.01 is the same as multiplying by 100.

Guided

$0.05 \times 0.0007 = 5 \times 10^{\ldots} \times 7 \times 10^{\ldots}$
$= 5 \times 7 \times 10^{\ldots + \ldots}$
$= 35 \times 10^{\ldots}$
$= 3.5 \times 10^{\ldots}$

$3.5 \times 10^{\ldots} \times 100 = 3.5 \times 10^{\ldots + 2}$
$= \ldots\ldots\ldots$

Top exam tip!

You need to spot square roots like $\sqrt{144} = 12$ without a calculator. Learn the square numbers up to 15^2.

Workout 3

4 Rounding, estimation and error

Warm up

✓ To round a number, look at the next digit to the right on a place value diagram:
- If it is 5 or more, round up
- If it is less than 5, round down

✓ The first digit in a number that is not zero is the first **significant figure (s.f.)**.

0.07**6**1 rounds to 0.08 to 1 s.f.

This is the first significant figure.

✓ To estimate an answer to a calculation, round each digit to 1 s.f.

✓ You can write an **error interval** for a rounded number. Here is the error interval for 2.90 rounded to 2 decimal places:

$$2.895 \leqslant x < 2.905$$

This is the smallest value that will round to 2.90

Use $\leqslant$ for the least possible value and $<$ for the greatest possible value.

Any value less than this will round to 2.90

Reps

1 Round 7256.5 to the nearest hundred. **7300**

a ten ....
b whole number ....
c thousand ....

2 Round to 1 significant figure.

2340   **2000**

a 0.251 ....
b 8.70 ....
c 345 ....
d 0.00372 ....

3 Estimate the answer by rounding each number.

2.1 × 37   **80**

a 5.5 × 8.9 ....
b 29.3 ÷ 4.5 ....
c 7.75^2 ....
d 391 × 0.470 ....

4 Write the missing number in each error interval.

$5.5 \leqslant x < 6.5$

a $8500 \leqslant x < $ ....
b .... $\leqslant x < 0.75$
c $10.5 \leqslant x < $ ....
d .... $\leqslant x < 3.05$

GCSE Maths: Bootcamp

Exam practice

1. Amir wants to buy 22 photo frames. Each photo frame costs £3.35.

   Amir does the calculation 20 × 3 = 60 to estimate the cost of the 22 photo frames.

   Explain how Amir's calculation shows that the actual cost will be more than £60. **(1 mark)**

   *If you have to **explain** something in your exam you should write an answer in words.*

   Guided Both values have been rounded ....

   So the actual answer will be .... than £60.

Links to: Pages 3, 10

2. Work out an estimate for
   $$\frac{221 \times 5.2}{0.185}$$ **(2 marks)**

   *Round each number to **1 significant figure** before working out the calculation. You can sometimes make a fraction calculation easier by multiplying the top and bottom by 10.*

   Guided $\frac{221 \times 5.2}{0.185} \approx \frac{200 \times ....}{............}$

   $= \frac{............}{............}$

   $= \frac{............}{............}$

   $= ....$

   You must use inequalities when writing down an error interval.

3. A number, n, is rounded to 1 decimal place. The result is 10.5.

   Write down the error interval for n.
   (2 marks)

   ....

Top exam tip!

Don't round values unless you are told to in a question, or you have to find an estimate.

Workout 4

5 Factors, multiples and primes

Warm up

- The **factors** of a number divide exactly into it. You can draw a factor tree to find the **prime factors** of a number.

- A **prime number** has exactly two factors: itself and 1.

  2, 3, 5, 7, 11 and 13 are all prime numbers.

- The **multiples** of a number are the numbers in its times table:

  6, 12, 18, 24 and 30 are all multiples of 6.

- The **highest common factor** of two numbers is the greatest number that is a factor of both numbers.

- The **lowest common multiple** of two numbers is the smallest number that is a multiple of both numbers.

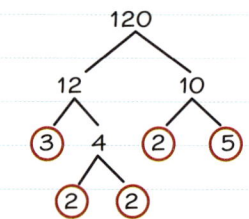

$120 = 2 \times 2 \times 2 \times 3 \times 5$
$= 2^3 \times 3 \times 5$

Reps

1 11, 12, 13, 14, 15, 16, 17, 18
From the list write down

   a multiple of 7 14
a a factor of 30 ....
b a multiple of 9 ....
c two multiples of 4 ....
d any prime numbers ....

2 Circle any prime factors of the given number in each list.

   12   1 ② ③ 4
a 28   4 7 14 28
b 39   1 3 9 13
c 45   3 5 9 15
d 100   2 5 10 50

3 a Fill in the Venn diagram to show the factors of 20 and the factors of 30.

   b Write down the highest common factor of 20 and 30.

   ....

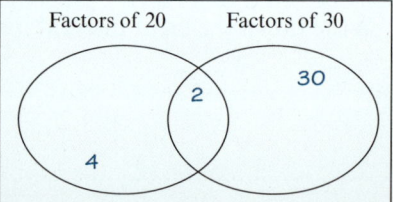

GCSE Maths: Bootcamp

Exam practice

 1. Becca says

'There are twice as many prime numbers between 10 and 20 as there are between 20 and 30.'

Is Becca correct? Show how you got your answer. **(2 marks)**

Guided

Prime numbers between 10 and 20:

11, ...

Prime numbers between 20 and 30:

23, ...

Conclusion:

....

so Becca is ....

 2. (a) Write 96 as a product of its prime factors. **(2 marks)**

....

(b) Find the highest common factor (HCF) of 96 and 30. **(2 marks)**

....

 **Links to:**
Pages 11, 12

Problem solved!
You need to show your working clearly. Write out all the prime numbers between 10 and 20, and all the prime numbers between 20 and 30, then write a **conclusion**.

Problem solved!
Make sure you **answer the question**. You need to state whether Becca is correct or incorrect.

Use a factor tree. Remember to stop each branch when you get to a prime number.

30 written as a product of prime factors is 2 × 3 × 5.

Top exam tip!
If you have to write a number as a **product** of prime factors, use × signs in your answer.

6 Algebra essentials

Warm up

✓ You can simplify expressions by **collecting like terms**. Like terms contain the same letters.

Like terms: xy $-3xy$ $+10xy$ $-xy$

Not like terms: $3a$ $+a^2$ $-2ab$ $-5a^2bc$

✓ You can use the index laws with powers of the same letter:

① $a^m \times a^n = a^{m+n}$ ② $(a^m)^n = a^{mn}$ ③ $\dfrac{a^m}{a^n} = a^{m-n}$

✓ To multiply or divide expressions in algebra you need to:

① Multiply or divide any number parts
② Multiply or divide the letter parts using the index laws

$x \times x^6 = x^{1+6} = x^7$

$7x \times 5x^6 = 35x^7$
  $7 \times 5 = 35$

$12 \div 3 = 4$

$\dfrac{12a^5}{3a^2} = 4a^3$

$a^5 \div a^2 = a^{5-2} = a^3$

Reps

1 Circle the pair of like terms in each list.

  $3x$ (${2xy}$) x^2 $5y$ (xy)
- **a** $2p$ $3q$ $5r$ $2pq$ $4r$
- **b** ab $2a^2$ $3b$ $2ab$ ab^2
- **c** $2m^2$ m^2n $5mn$ m^2 $3m$
- **d** $3xy$ $2x^2y$ xy^2 $2x$ x^2y

2 Simplify by collecting like terms.

  $7a + b - 3a + 2b$ $4a + 3b$
- **a** $10x - 6x$ ....
- **b** $4p + 2p - p$ ....
- **c** $7m + n + 3n + m$ ....
- **d** $4a - b + 2a - 5b$ ....

3 Use the index laws to simplify.

  $y^3 \times y^4$ y^7
- **a** $a^4 \times a$ ....
- **b** $(c^2)^3$ ....
- **c** $\dfrac{x^{10}}{x^2}$ ....
- **d** $\dfrac{b^2 \times b^{10}}{b^3}$ ....

4 Match the simplified expressions.

  $x^2 \times 2xy$ $8x^2y^2$
- **a** $4x \times 2xy^2$ $2xy$
- **b** $2x^2y \times xy^2$ $2x^3y$
- **c** $\dfrac{2x^2y}{x}$ $4x^2y^3$
- **d** $x^2y \times 4y^2$ $2x^3y^3$

GCSE Maths: Bootcamp

 **Exam practice**

1. (a) Simplify $10x - 3x + x$ **(1 mark)**

....

(b) Simplify $n^2 + n^2 + n^2$ **(1 mark)**

$n^2 + n^2 + n^2$ means 'three lots of n^2'.

....

(c) Simplify $4p - 5q - p + 6 - 2q$ **(2 marks)**

The term $+ 6$ should still appear in your final answer.

....

(d) Simplify $\dfrac{3y + 5y}{2}$ **(1 mark)**

Start by simplifying $3y + 5y$.

....

Problem solved!

2. $(3x + y)$ cm

$2y$ cm

Write an expression for the perimeter of this rectangle. Simplify your answer.

(3 marks)

The **perimeter** is the distance all the way around the shape. Add together expressions for **all four** sides, then simplify your answer. Remember that opposite sides of a rectangle are equal.

 Guided $(3x + y) + 2y + (3x + y) + 2y$

= ....x + ...y

.... cm

 3. Simplify $(2ab^2)^3$ **(3 marks)**

Powers apply to **everything** inside the brackets. So this is the same as $2^3 \times a^3 \times (b^2)^3$

....

Workout 6

7 Brackets and factorising

Warm up

- To expand brackets you multiply the term outside the brackets by **every term** inside the brackets.
- Each term takes the sign (+ or –) in front of it.
- Factorising is the opposite of expanding brackets.

$$2x(x + 3) = 2x^2 + 6x$$

Expanding brackets / Factorising

- To expand two brackets you can use a grid, or the FOIL method. FOIL stands for **F**irst, **O**uter, **I**nner, **L**ast:

	x	-4
x	x^2	$-4x$
$+3$	$+3x$	-12

$$(x + 3)(x - 4) = x^2 - 4x + 3x - 12$$
$$= x^2 - x - 12$$

$x^2 - 4x + 3x - 12 = x^2 - x - 12$

- To factorise an expression in the form $x^2 + bx + c$ you need to find two numbers that **add up to b**, and that **multiply to make c**.

Reps

1 Expand

$3x(x + 4)$ $3x^2 + 12$

a) $6(n + 2)$ ....
b) $a(2a + b)$ ....
c) $5x(2 - x)$ ....
d) $2p(3q + 2p^2)$ ....

2 Factorise fully

$10 - 5x$ $5(2 - x)$

a) $2m + 6$ ....
b) $10a^2 - 2a$ ....
c) $x^2 + 3x$ ....
d) $2x^3 - 4xy$ ....

3 Expand and simplify

$(x + 1)(x + 3)$ $x^2 + 4x + 3$

a) $n(2 + n) + 3n$ ....
b) $5(p + 1) - 2(1 - p)$ ....
c) $(y + 1)(y - 3)$ ....
d) $(e - 2)(e - 5)$ ....

4 Factorise

$x^2 + 6x + 5$ $(x + 1)(x + 5)$

a) $x^2 + 3x + 2$ ....
b) $y^2 - 4y + 3$ ....
c) $n^2 + 6n + 9$ ....
d) $x^2 - x - 6$ ....

GCSE Maths: Bootcamp

Exam practice

1. Expand and simplify $5(2x - 1) - 4(x + 3)$
(2 marks)

> Be careful with the minus sign in the second pair of brackets. Multiply −4 by x to get −4x, and multiply −4 by 3 to get −12.

....

2. Expand and simplify $(2x + 1)(x + 3)$
(2 marks)

Guided

	x	+ 3
2x		+ 6x
+ 1		

> You can use a grid method like the one shown, or you could use FOIL. Your final answer should have one x^2 term, one x term and one number term.

.... + 6x + ... + ...

= .... + ... + ...

3. Factorise fully
(a) $4y^2 + 10y$ **(2 marks)**

> To factorise fully, look for the largest factor of both terms in the expression.

Guided

= $2(2y^2 + \ldots\ldots y)$

= $\ldots\ldots(2y + \ldots\ldots)$

(b) $x^2 + 7x + 10$ **(3 marks)**

> You need to find two numbers that add up to 7 and multiply to make 10. Your answer will look like $(x + \ldots)(x + \ldots)$.

Top exam tip!

Check factorisations by expanding the brackets.

....

Workout 7

8 Equations and inequalities

Warm up

✓ You can **solve** a linear equation by rearranging the equation so the unknown is on its own on one side. Follow these steps when solving a linear equation:

| Multiply through to get rid of any fractions | → | Expand any brackets and simplify | → | Add or subtract number parts and multiples of x | → | Divide by the number in front of x to get x on its own |

✓ The **solution** to an inequality tells you the range of values of x that **satisfy** the inequality.

✓ When solving a linear inequality, if you multiply or divide by a **negative number** you have to **reverse** the inequality.

Reps

1 Solve

$4x = 8$ $x = 2$

a $x - 12 = 3$ $x = $ ....

b $2x = 5$ $x = $ ....

c $x + 9 = 4$ $x = $ ....

d $\frac{x}{6} = 3.5$ $x = $ ....

2 Solve

$4x + 3 = 19$ $x = 4$

a $10x - 10 = 60$ $x = $ ....

b $2x + 1 = 6x - 9$ $x = $ ....

c $8 - 8x = 20 - 2x$ $x = $ ....

d $2(x - 3) = 7$ $x = $ ....

3 Write down all the integers that satisfy each inequality.

$-2 < x \leq 1$ $-1, 0, 1$

a $3 < x < 7$ ....

b $-5 \leq x < -3$ ....

c $0 \leq x \leq 3$ ....

d $10 < x < 15$ ....

4 Solve each inequality.

$x - 4 > 3$ $x > 7$

a $2x < 10$ ....

b $x + 8 \geq 2$ ....

c $3x - 2 \leq 10$ ....

d $x + 1 \geq 2x + 5$ ....

GCSE Maths: Bootcamp

Exam practice

1. $-1 \leq n < 4$

n is an integer. Write down all the possible values of n. **(2 marks)**

> Integers are whole numbers, **including 0**.
> $\leq$ means that you include -1, but $<$ means that you **don't** include 4.

....

2. Solve $\dfrac{2x+1}{3} = x - 7$ **(3 marks)**

> Start by multiplying everything by 3 to get rid of the fraction.

$x =$ ....

3. Find the area of this square.

$(3x - 5)$ cm

$(x + 2)$ cm

(4 marks)

Problem solved!

You can form your own equation and solve it to find the value of x. Use the fact that all four sides of a square are the same length.

 Guided

$3x - 5 = x + 2$

$3x = x + \ldots\ldots$

$\ldots\ldots x = \ldots\ldots$

$x = \ldots\ldots$

Side length = ...

So area = ...

.... cm^2

Top exam tip!

Make sure you answer the question. Here, your final answer should be the **area** of the square, not the value of x.

9 Formulae

Warm up

✓ A formula is a rule used to work out the value of one letter by **substituting** the values of other letters.

✓ The letter on its own on one side of the equals sign is called the **subject**.

✓ You can **rearrange** a formula to make a different letter the subject.

M is the subject
$$M = 3A + 5 \quad (-5)$$
$$M - 5 = 3A \quad (\div 3)$$
$$\frac{M-5}{3} = A$$
A is the subject

✓ You need to know the difference between an expression, an equation and a formula:

$7x + 10y$	$2x + 1 = 9$	$F = ma$
This **expression** has two **terms** and no = sign	This **equation** has **one unknown** and an = sign	This **formula** has **more than one unknown** and an = sign

Reps

1 Write 'expression', 'equation' or 'formula'.

$4a + 2b$ — expression

a $2y = 8$ ....
b $10x^2 - 1$ ....
c $p = 2q + 1$ ....
d $x = 2x - 5$ ....

2 If $x = 2$ and $y = 5$, find the value of

$2x + 3y$ — 19

a $10y + 1$ ....
b $2y - x$ ....
c $15x - y^2$ ....
d $5x + xy$ ....

3 Make Q the subject of each formula.

$P = 10Q + R \qquad Q = \dfrac{P - R}{10}$

a $P = Q + 50$
....

b $P = \dfrac{Q + 1}{5}$
....

c $P = 10R - 5Q$
....

d $P = 2QR + 5$
....

GCSE Maths: Bootcamp

Exam practice

1. | expression equation formula identity
     inequality term factor multiple |

Choose two words from the box to make a correct statement.

$2x$ is a .... in the

.... $2x - y$ **(2 marks)**

Read the sentence back to yourself to check your answer.

2. This path is made up of 6 identical rectangular pavers of length x, and one paver of length 4. The total length of the path is L. All measurements are in metres.

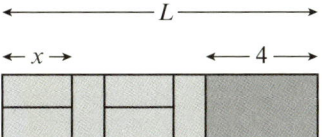

Find a formula for L in terms of x. Write your formula as simply as possible. **(3 marks)**

Problem solved!

*You don't know the **width** of the smaller pavers, but you can work it out from the diagram.*

Your answer is a formula so it should start $L = ...$

....

3. $P = \sqrt{y + 10}$

(a) Work out the value of P when $y = 15$ **(2 marks)**

Guided $P = \sqrt{15 + 10} = \sqrt{.........} = ...$

$P = ...$

(b) Make y the subject of the formula $P = \sqrt{y + 10}$ **(2 marks)**

*In part (b), the first operation is to **square** both sides to get rid of the square root.*

Top exam tip!

Use BIDMAS to remember the correct order of operations when substituting.

....

10 Sequences

Warm up

✓ An **arithmetic** sequence has a constant difference between terms.

✓ The **nth term** tells you how to find each term using the term number.

✓ To find the nth term, look at **multiples** of the **common difference** and compare them to each term in the sequence.

✓ Number sequence ✓ Pattern sequence

Common difference

10   13   16   19   22   ...

Multiples of 3 are 3, 6, 9, 12, 15

nth term = 3n + 7

1 dot   5 dots   9 dots

nth term = 4n − 3

Reps

1 Find the next two terms in each sequence.

    2   5   8   11   14   **17   20**
a −1   4   9   14   19   ....
b 100   90   80   70   ....
c 1   2   3   5   8   ....
d 1   4   9   16   25   ....

2 Write the rule to get from one term to the next.

    10   7   4   1   −2   **subtract 3**
a 5   7   9   11   13   ......
b 10   15   20   25   ......
c 14   8   2   −4   ......
d 3   6   12   24   48   ......

3 Write the first three terms in these sequences with an nth term.

    6n − 5   **1   7   13**
a 3n + 10   ....
b 20 − 2n   ....
c n^3 ....
d $2n^2$ ....

4 Find the nth term of each arithmetic sequence.

    1   3   5   7   9   **2n − 1**
a 2   4   6   8   10   ......
b 10   15   20   25   30   ......
c −1   5   11   17   23   ......
d 1   10   19   28   37   ......

GCSE Maths: Bootcamp

Exam practice

1. Here are the first six terms of an arithmetic sequence.

    4   11   18   25   32   39

Find an expression, in terms of n, for the nth term of this sequence. **(2 marks)**

 Common difference = ...

Multiples of .... are ....

nth term = ...n − ....

> Start by finding the common difference. This is how much the sequence goes up by each time. Work out what you have to do to each multiple of this number to get a term in the sequence.

2. The nth term in an arithmetic sequence is $6n - 1$.

Is 103 a term in this sequence?
Show how you get your answer. **(2 marks)**

> For every term in the sequence, n must be a **whole number**. Try solving $6n - 1 = 103$ to see if you get a whole-number answer.

3. The rule to get from one term to the next term in a sequence is

> Add k then multiply by 2

The first term is 7 and the second term is 20.
Find the third term in the sequence.
(3 marks)

Problem solved!

You need to start by finding the value of k.

Top exam tip!

Try some numbers to see what is going on. Imagine the rule is 'Add 1 then multiply by 2', and see what the second term would be.

....

Links to:
Pages
34–35

11 Coordinates and lines

Warm up

✓ Coordinates are written (x, y). The first number shows the horizontal position and the second number shows the vertical position.

✓ Horizontal lines have equation
$y = \square$

✓ Vertical lines have equation
$x = \square$

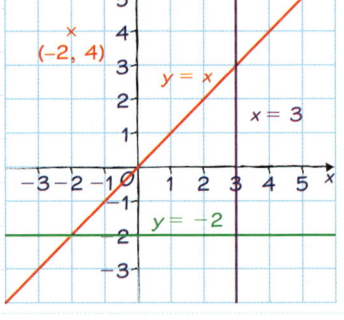

✓ The equation of a straight line can be written as $y = mx + c$.
The **gradient** is m and the **y-intercept** is $(0, c)$.

✓ Parallel lines have the same gradient.

Reps

1 Write down the coordinates of each point.

$P = (-1, -2)$
a. $Q = (....., ...)$
b. $R = (....., ...)$
c. $S = (....., ...)$
d. $T = (....., ...)$

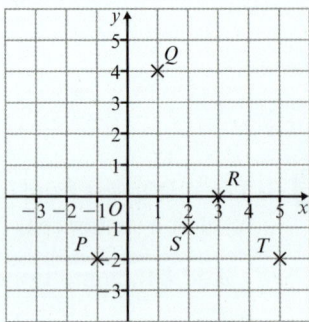

2 Match each line to the correct equation.

A $y = x + 4$
B $y = 2x - 1$
C $y = 1$
D $x = 4$
E $y = -x$

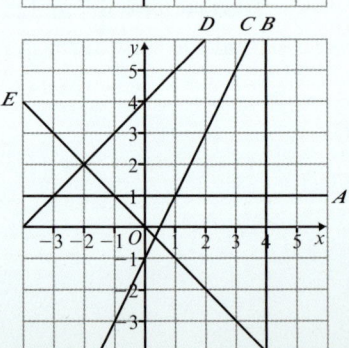

GCSE Maths: Bootcamp

Exam practice

1. The diagram shows three identical squares.

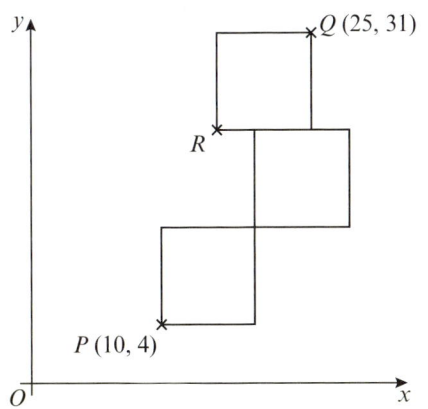

Work out the coordinates of point *R*. **(4 marks)**

(..............., ...)

Links to: Pages 36–39

Problem solved!

The diagram is not drawn to scale so you can't measure.

The height of three squares is 31 − 4 = 27. Use this to work out the height of one square. Then work out how to change the coordinates of point Q to get the coordinates of point R.

2. A straight line passes through the points (0, −2) and (3, 7).
Find an equation of the line. **(4 marks)**

Guided

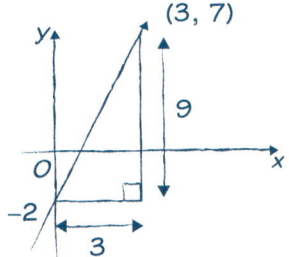

Gradient = $\frac{9}{3}$ = ...

y-intercept = ...

y = ...x − ....

To find the gradient of a line, draw a right-angled triangle and work out $\frac{\text{distance up}}{\text{distance across}}$

Top exam tip!

If no diagram is given with a question you can draw a sketch to see what is going on.

Workout 11

12 Real-life graphs

Warm up

- ✓ Graphs showing direct proportion are straight lines through the origin.
- ✓ You can write the relationship as $y = kx$, where k is the gradient of the graph.
- ✓ On a **distance–time** graph, gradient represents speed.
- ✓ On a **velocity–time** graph, gradient represents acceleration.

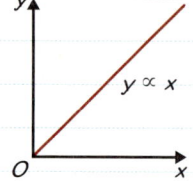

Reps

1 The diagram shows a travel graph for an orienteering competition.

Find the speed of the competitor in section **A**.   2.5 km/h

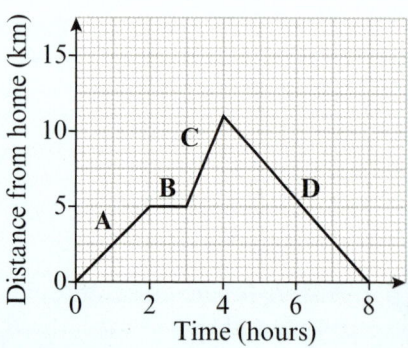

a section **B** .... km/h
b section **C** .... km/h
c section **D** .... km/h

2 In which section was the competitor

leaving home   A
a returning home ....
b travelling fastest ....
c not moving ....

3 Write down the letter that describes each velocity–time graph.

a Decelerating   b Stationary   c Constant speed   d Accelerating

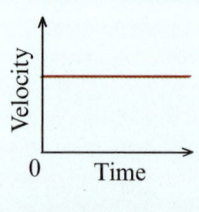 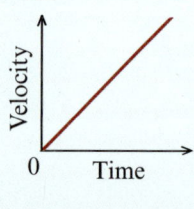 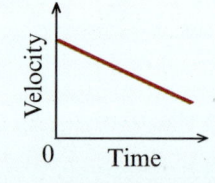 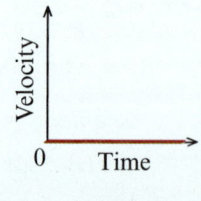

....   a   ....

GCSE Maths: Bootcamp

Exam practice

1. You can use this graph to convert between kilograms and pounds.

> To read off the graph, read up from 34 kg on the horizontal axis, then read across to the vertical axis.

Guided

> When reading graphs make sure you are correct to the nearest **small square**.

(a) Change 34 kg into lb. **(1 mark)**

.... lb

1 tonne = 1000 kg

(b) Explain how you could use your answer to convert 3.4 tonnes into lb. **(2 marks)**

> The graph doesn't go up to 3400 on the horizontal axis. Think how you could use proportion to find the answer, then describe your method in words.

....

....

Alice says that the graph shows that kilograms are directly proportional to pounds.

(c) Is Alice correct? Explain your answer. **(1 mark)**

....

....

Top exam tip!

Draw lines on your graphs with a ruler and pencil. This helps you **show your working** and also makes it easier to read accurately.

Workout 12

13 Curvy graphs

Warm up

✓ A quadratic graph has an x^2 term. It has a **turning point**, with a vertical **line of symmetry** through that point.

✓ The points where $y = x^2 - 6x$ crosses the x-axis are the solutions to the quadratic equation $x^2 - 6x = 0$. The x-coordinate of the turning point is halfway between these points.

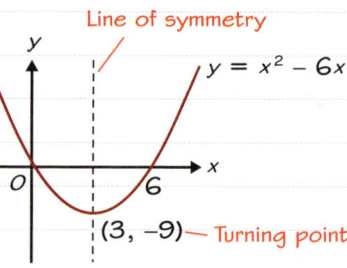

✓ Here are three other types of graph you need to be able to recognise:

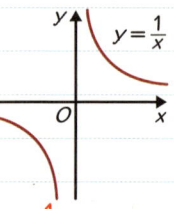

$y = \frac{1}{x}$ is a **reciprocal** graph.

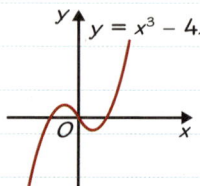

A **cubic graph** has an x^3 term in its equation.

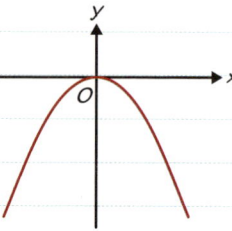

This is the graph of $y = -x^2$.

Reps

1 Write 'curvy' or 'straight' next to each equation to describe the graph.

$y = 3x$ straight

a $y = x^2$ ....   b $y = 10 - x$ ....

c $x = 5$ ....   d $y = x^3 + 2$ ....

2 For each graph, write down the letter of the matching equation.

A $y = 3 - x$ **B** $y = 10 - x^2$ **C** $y = x^3 - x^2$ **D** $y = \frac{1}{2}x - 1$

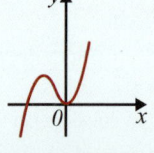
....

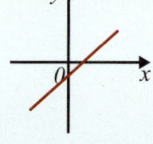
....

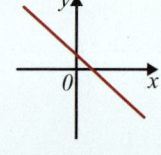
A

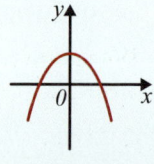
....

Exam practice

1. (a) On the grid, draw the graph of
$y = x^2 + 2x - 1$
You can use the table of values to help you.

x	–3	–2	–1	0	1
y	2	–1			

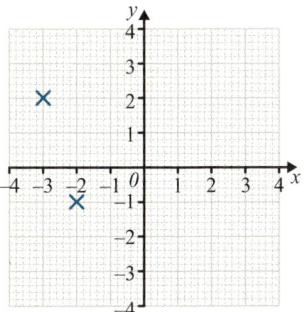

(3 marks)

(b) Write down the coordinates of the turning point of the graph. **(1 mark)**

(.............., ...)

(c) Write down the solutions to
$x^2 + 2x - 1 = 0$ **(2 marks)**

....

2. Steven has drawn part of a graph of
$y = x - \frac{1}{10}x^3$

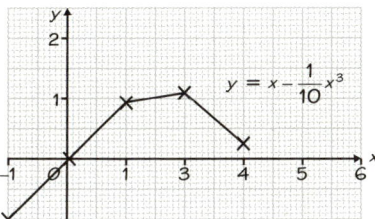

Write down two things that are wrong with Steven's graph. **(2 marks)**

....

....

It's sometimes easier to draw a curve if you turn the paper and place your hand **inside** the curve.

The solutions are the x-coordinates of the points where the curve crosses the x-axis. Read the values off the graph accurate to the **nearest small square**.

Top exam tip!

Graphs of curves should always be drawn with a **sharp pencil** in a **single, smooth curve**. Top mistakes to avoid are joining points with straight lines, or drawing 'hairy' graphs with lots of short lines.

Links to:
Pages 44–45, 48

14 Tricky algebra

Warm up

✓ You can tackle these tricky algebra topics when you are feeling confident with your other algebra skills.

✓ You can write an odd number as $2n + 1$, and an even number as $2n$, where n is an integer.

	Product	Sum
Odd & odd	odd	even
Odd & even	even	odd
Even & even	even	even

✓ Equations of the form $x^2 + bx + c = 0$ are called **quadratic equations**. If you can **factorise** the left-hand side, you can set each factor equal to zero to find the solutions.

✓ The solutions to a pair of **simultaneous equations** are values that make **both equations** true at the same time:

Multiply one or both equations to make one pair of coefficients equal ⇒ Add or subtract the equations to eliminate one of the variables ⇒ Solve, then substitute back into one equation to find the value of the other variable

Reps

1 Assuming k is an integer, write odd or even for each expression.
$2k + 1$ **odd**
- **a** $10k$ ....
- **b** $k(k + 1)$ ....
- **c** $4k + 5$ ....
- **d** $k + (k + 3)$ ....

2 Write down the solutions to each factorised quadratic equation.
$(x + 1)(x - 5) = 0$ $x = -1$ or 5
- **a** $(x - 4)(x - 3) = 0$ $x = ...$ or $......$
- **b** $(x + 2)(x + 2) = 0$ $x = ...$
- **c** $(x + 1)(x - 7) = 0$ $x = ...$ or $......$
- **d** $(x + 4)(x - 2) = 0$ $x = ...$ or $......$

3 Multiply every term in each linear equation by 2.
$2y + 3x = 1$ $4y + 6x = 2$
- **a** $x - 4y = 2$ ....
- **b** $3x + 5y = 7$ ....
- **c** $2x = 6y + 1$ ....
- **d** $y = 3 - x$ ....

GCSE Maths: Bootcamp

Exam practice

1. Solve $x^2 + 4x - 21 = 0$ **(3 marks)**

Guided
$(x + \ldots\ldots)(x - \ldots\ldots) = 0$

When $x + \ldots\ldots = 0$, $x = \ldots\ldots\ldots$

When $x - \ldots\ldots = 0$, $x = \ldots\ldots\ldots$

Solution is $x = \ldots\ldots\ldots$ or $x = \ldots\ldots\ldots$

> Factorise the left-hand side, then set each factor equal to 0. There are **two solutions**.

2. (a) Use algebra to show that the sum of two odd numbers is always an even number. **(2 marks)**

Problem solved!

> Write the two odd numbers as $2n + 1$ and $2m + 1$. Then add them together. Show that the resulting expression must have a factor of 2.

x and y are consecutive whole numbers.
(b) Explain why their sum will always be an odd number. **(2 marks)**

....

....

3. Solve the simultaneous equations
$x + y = 6$
$2x - 4y = 3$ **(3 marks)**

> Number the simultaneous equations ① and ②. Then look for a way to make one pair of coefficients equal. Multiply equation ① by 2 to get $2x + 2y = 12$. You can then subtract equation ② to **eliminate x**.

$x = \ldots\ldots\ldots\ldots\ldots\ldots$

$y = \ldots\ldots\ldots\ldots\ldots\ldots$

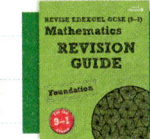
Links to: Pages 47, 49, 51, 52

Top exam tip!

If you can't see how to start a question, skip it and come back to it later.

Workout 14

15 Percentages

Warm up

✓ Learn these common fraction, decimal and percentage equivalents:

Fraction	$\frac{1}{100}$	$\frac{1}{10}$	$\frac{1}{5}$	$\frac{1}{4}$	$\frac{1}{2}$	$\frac{3}{4}$
Decimal	0.01	0.1	0.2	0.25	0.5	0.75
Percentage	1%	10%	20%	25%	50%	75%

✓ To find a percentage of an amount, divide by 100 to find 1%, then multiply by the percentage.

✓ To write one quantity as a percentage of another quantity, divide the first quantity by the second quantity, then multiply by 100.

✓ Use a **multiplier** to find a percentage increase or decrease.

✓ If you are given a final amount, divide by the multiplier to find the original amount.

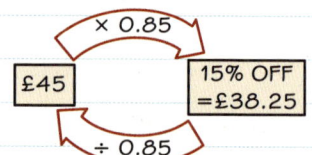

Reps

1 Find

10% of £300 — £30
a) 20% of 600 g — .... g
b) 5% of 80 km — .... km
c) 75% of 2 kg — .... kg
d) 43% of 7200 ml — .... ml

2 Write each amount as a percentage of £2500

£500 — 20%
a) £1250 — .... %
b) £1000 — .... %
c) £300 — .... %
d) £1700 — .... %

3 Write the correct multiplier.

10% increase — 1.1
a) 50% increase — ....
b) 20% decrease — ....
c) 3% increase — ....
d) 42% decrease — ....

4 Increase each amount by 35%.

£200 — £270
a) 50 g — .... g
b) 1.8 m — .... m
c) 90 kg — .... kg
d) 1000 km — .... km

GCSE Maths: Bootcamp

Exam practice

1. (a) Write $\frac{3}{5}$ as a percentage. **(1 mark)**

   ....%

   (b) Write 0.85 as a percentage. **(1 mark)**

   ....%

Links to: Pages 55–58, 62

$\frac{1}{5}$ is 20%, so multiply this by 3.

To find the multiplier for a 5% **increase** work out $\frac{100 + 5}{100}$

2. All the employees at a company receive a 5% pay rise.

   (a) Paula was paid £1800 per month **before** the pay rise. Work out her monthly pay after the pay rise. **(2 marks)**

   Guided
   Multiplier for 5% increase = ………
   1800 × …….. = …………

   £……………

   (b) Dhruv was paid £1470 **after** the pay rise. Work out his monthly pay before the pay rise. **(2 marks)**

   £……………

To find the **original amount** before the percentage change, divide 1470 by the multiplier.

Problem solved!

Read word problems carefully. Here you are asked to find the percentage profit. To do this:
- find the total selling price
- work out the profit in pounds
- divide the profit by the **original cost** and multiply by 100%

3. Jaden buys 20 bars of chocolate for a total of £7.95
   She sells all 20 bars for 60p each.
   Work out Jaden's percentage profit. Give your answer to 1 decimal place. **(3 marks)**

   Total selling price: 20 × …… = £……..
   Profit: ……… − 7.95 = £……..
   Percentage profit:

   $\frac{\ldots\ldots}{7.95} \times 100 = \ldots\ldots\ldots\%$

   ....%

Top exam tip!

Work in **either** pounds or pence, but not both!

Workout 15

16 Ratio and proportion

Warm up

✓ Simplify a ratio by dividing each part by the same whole number.

10 : 18 ÷2 ÷2 → 5 : 9

✓ To divide a number in a given ratio

| Work out the total number of parts in the ratio | → | Divide the amount by the total parts to find the value of one part | → | Multiply the value of one part by each part in the ratio to find the amounts | → | Check the amounts add to the correct total |

✓ Two quantities are in **direct proportion** if one doubles when the other doubles.

✓ Two quantities are in **inverse proportion** if one doubles when the other halves.

Reps

1 Write these ratios in simplest form.

12 : 18   **2 : 3**

a 5 : 10   ....
b 25 : 10   ....
c 2 : 10 : 12   ....
d 12 : 30 : 15 ....

2 Divide £600 in the ratio

2 : 1   **£400 and £200**

a 1 : 3   £............ and £............
b 5 : 1   £............ and £............
c 5 : 7   £............ and £............
d 1 : 9   £............ and £............

3 y is directly proportional to x. When $y = 3$, $x = 10$. Find

y when $x = 20$ **6**

a y when $x = 5$ ....
b x when $y = 15$ ....
c y when $x = 100$ ....
d y when $x = 8$ ....

4 12 kg of potatoes cost £9.12 Find the cost of

3 kg   **£2.28**

a 1 kg   ....
b 5 kg   ....
c 15 kg   ....
d 750 g   ....

GCSE Maths: Bootcamp

Exam practice

Links to:
Pages 59–60, 67

1. A jar of biscuits contains only ginger nuts, chocolate digestives and plain digestives, in the ratio 6 : 5 : 9
   Work out what percentage of the biscuits are ginger nuts. **(2 marks)**

   ....%

   > Work out the total number of parts in the ratio. The **fraction** of biscuits that are ginger nuts is 6 divided by this number. Write the fraction then convert it into a percentage.

2. Alison is 2 years younger than Christina. The sum of their ages is 30.
   Find the ratio of Alison's age to Christina's age. Give your answer in its simplest form. **(3 marks)**

   Problem solved!
   Write Alison's age as a and Christina's age as $a + 2$. Then solve an equation to find a.

   Guided
   $a + (a + 2) = 30$

   .... = 30

   ....

   $a = ...$

   Alison : Christina = ... : ....

   = ... : ....

3. A brand of cereal is sold in two different-sized boxes

   | Standard size (500 g): £1.50 |
   | Family size (750 g): £2.10 |

   Which box offers the better value? Give reasons for your answer. **(3 marks)**

   Problem solved!
   You need to show enough working to justify your answer. You could work out what **one** gram (or 50 g) of cereal costs for each option.

   Top exam tip!
   If you have to choose between two options, make sure you **write down** the option you have chosen. Don't just circle or underline it.

Workout 16

17 Measuring and estimating

Warm up

✓ To convert between metric units multiply by 10, 100 or 1000:

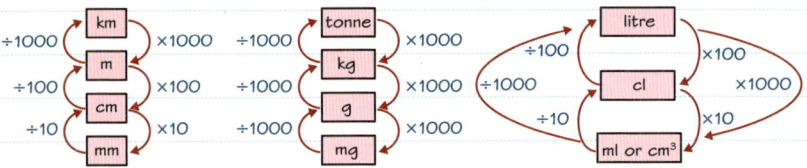

✓ To read a scale you need to work out what each **small division** represents.

✓ Use a **protractor** in your exam to measure angles to the nearest degree.

✓ In the 24-hour clock you **add 12** to times after 12 pm (midday).
1 pm = 1300   10 pm = 2200

✓ Use a **ruler** in your exam to measure lines to the nearest mm.

Reps

1 Convert

   0.2 m into cm   20 cm
a 65 cm into m   ………… m
b 0.15 litres into ml   ………… ml
c 2400 g into kg   ………… kg
d 420 m into km   ………… km

2 Write each time in the 24-hour clock.

   9.30 am   09:30
a 2.15 pm   …………………
b 12.45 am   …………………
c 7.20 pm   …………………
d 11.05 pm   …………………

3 Measure each line to the nearest mm.

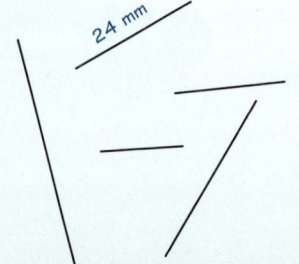

4 Label each reading on the scale.

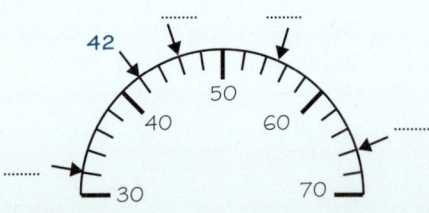

Exam practice

1. The diagram shows a house and a man. The man is average height. The house and the man are drawn to the same scale.

Links to: Pages 61, 77–78, 95–96

   (a) Write down an estimate for the real height of the man in metres. **(1 mark)**

   .... m

Problem solved!
You need to use common sense to write down an estimate for the height of the man. Any height between 1.5 m and 2 m would be a reasonable estimate.

   (b) Work out an estimate for the real height of the house in metres. **(2 marks)**

Guided

Drawing: Height of house = ... × height of man

Real life: Height of house = ... × ....

= .... m

Work out how many times taller the house is than the man on the scale drawing. Then multiply your estimate by this.

2. This is part of a train timetable from Leeds to Bingley.

Leeds	08:40	09:10	09:33	09:59
Shipley	08:53	09:23	09:48	10:12
Bingley	09:00	09:27	09:52	10:17

   (a) Ashley says that the 09:59 train is the quickest from Leeds to Bingley. Is she correct? Explain your answer. **(1 mark)**

Read down the timetable and work out how long each train takes to get from Leeds to Bingley. Then write a conclusion.

....

Deepak lives in Leeds and works in Bingley. It takes him 18 minutes to walk to Leeds train station and 5 minutes to buy a ticket.

Count back 18 minutes then 5 minutes from 09:10

   (b) What is the latest he can leave home if he wants to catch the 09:10 train? **(2 marks)**

....

Top exam tip!
Remember your ruler. Measure lengths on scale drawings – don't guess them!

Workout 17

18 Compound measures

Warm up

✓ This is the formula triangle for **speed**, **distance** and **time**:

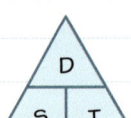

$S = \frac{D}{T}$ $D = S \times T$ $T = \frac{D}{S}$

✓ This is the formula triangle for **density**, **mass** and **volume**:

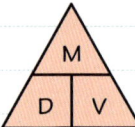

$D = \frac{M}{V}$ $M = D \times V$ $V = \frac{M}{D}$

✓ To convert units of area use a length multiplier **squared**.
✓ To convert units of volume use a length multiplier **cubed**.

Reps

1 Write 'speed', 'density' or 'pressure' after each unit.

kg/m³ .... density

a) km/h ....
b) N/cm² ....
c) g/cm³ ....
d) m/s ....

2 A cyclist travels 30 km. Work out her average speed if she takes

2 hours .... 15 km/h

a) 6 hours .... km/h
b) 2.5 hours .... km/h
c) 90 minutes .... km/h
d) $1\frac{1}{4}$ hours .... km/h

3 Complete the missing values in the table.

	Mass (g)	Volume (cm³)	Density (g/cm³)
	12	1.5	8
a	100	8	....
b	660	....	2.2
c	....	250	1.6

4 Convert

2 cm² into mm²   200 mm²

a) 0.8 m² into cm²   .... cm²
b) 300 mm³ into cm³   .... cm³
c) 0.025 km² into m²   .... m²
d) 0.004 m³ into cm³   .... cm³

GCSE Maths: Bootcamp

Exam practice

Links to: Pages 64–66, 85

1. An iron block has a mass of 280 g. The density of iron is 7.9 g/cm³.
Work out the volume of the block.
Give your answer correct to 1 decimal place. **(2 marks)**

> Look at the formula triangle for density. You want to find volume so cover up V. The position of the other letters tells you the formula:
> $V = \dfrac{M}{D}$

.... cm³

> If you are entering mixed numbers on your calculator it is easier to convert them to decimals first. $1\tfrac{1}{2} = 1.5$

2. Two friends drove at a constant speed on the M8 from Glasgow to Edinburgh. Hamid took $1\tfrac{1}{2}$ hours to complete the 75 km journey.
Chloe started her journey 15 minutes after Hamid, and caught up with him 45 minutes later.
Work out Chloe's speed, correct to 1 decimal place. **(5 marks)**

Problem solved!

> If you can't spot a complete strategy for the question, think about what you **can** work out easily. You know Hamid's time and distance, so you can calculate his speed.

Guided

Hamid's speed = $\dfrac{D}{T}$ = $\dfrac{............}{............}$ = ...

After 1 hour he had travelled .... km

Chloe's speed =

Top exam tip!

> Make sure your units are consistent before you use the formulae for speed or density.

.... km/h

Workout 18

19 All the angles

Warm up

  Learn these angle facts:
- Alternate angles are equal ($a = b$)
- Corresponding angles are equal ($a = c$)
- Vertically opposite angles are equal ($b = c$)
- Allied angles add up to 180° ($a + d = 180°$)
- Angles around a point add up to 360° ($b + c + d + e = 360°$)
- Angles on a straight line add up to 180° ($b + d = 180°$)
- Opposite angles in a parallelogram are equal ($b = f$)

  In a regular n-sided polygon:
- Sum of interior angles = $180° \times (n - 2)$
- Sum of exterior angles = $360°$, so each exterior angle = $\dfrac{360°}{n}$

Reps

1 Write in the missing angles on this diagram.

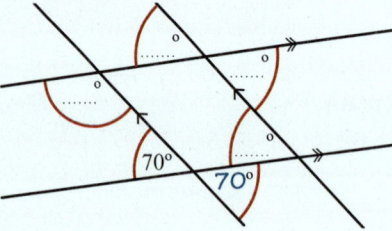

2 Write in the missing angles on this diagram.

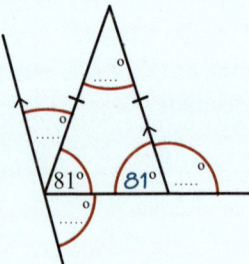

3 Complete the missing values in the table showing angles in regular polygons.

Number of sides	Interior angle	Exterior angle
6	120°	60°
4	........°	........°
8	........°	........°
....	........°	18°

GCSE Maths: Bootcamp

Exam practice

1. In the diagram, *ABFE* is a parallelogram. *BCD* and *DEF* are straight lines.

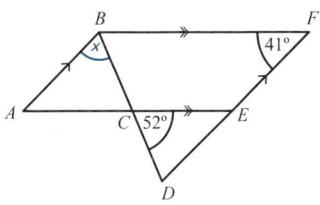

Angle *DCE* = 52° and angle *BFE* = 41°.
Show that angle *ABC* = 87°. **(4 marks)**

Angle ACB = ...

Reason: ....

Angle BAC = ...

Reason: ....

So .... + ... + x = 180°

Reason: ....

x = 180° – .... = ...

> Angles are labelled with the vertex in the middle. Angle ABC has been marked with an x on the diagram.

> **Problem solved!**
> **Show** all your working and write down the angle facts you use.

> Write in angles on the diagram as you work them out.

2. The diagram shows a hexagon. The two angles marked *x* are equal in size. Work out the value of *x*.

(5 marks)

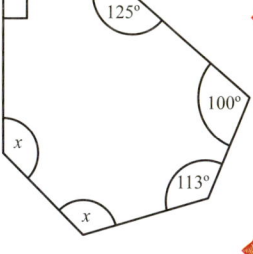

> Use 180° × (n – 2) to work out the sum of the interior angles.

> **Problem solved!**
> Add up the angles you know and subtract this from the sum of the interior angles. Then divide by 2.

x = ...°

> **Top exam tip!**
> Don't be afraid to write your own equation and solve it!

Links to: Pages 73–76

20 Perimeter and area

Warm up

✓ The **perimeter** is the distance all the way around a 2D shape, and the **area** is the amount of space it takes up.

✓ You need to learn these four area formulae:

1 Rectangle

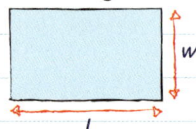

Area = $l \times w$

2 Parallelogram

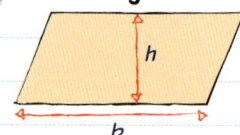

Area = $b \times h$

3 Triangle

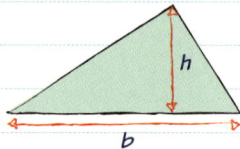

Area = $\frac{1}{2} \times b \times h$

4 Trapezium

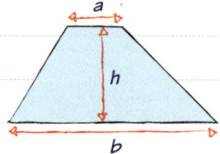

Area = $\frac{1}{2} \times (a + b) \times h$

Reps

1 Fill in the missing values.

a

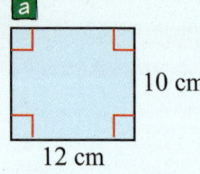

Area = $120 \, cm^2$

Perimeter = ... cm

b

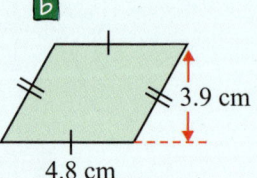

Area = ... cm^2

Perimeter = ... cm

c

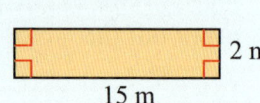

Area = ... m^2

Perimeter = ... m

d

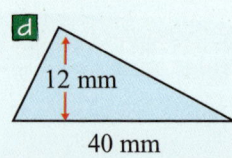

Area = ... mm^2

e

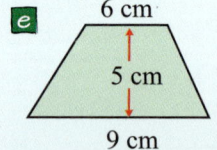

Area = ... cm^2

f

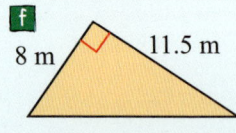

Area = ... m^2

GCSE Maths: Bootcamp

Exam practice

1. This triangle and rectangle have the same area. **(1 mark)**

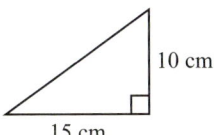
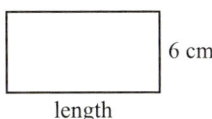

Find the length of the rectangle. **(3 marks)**

Guided Area of triangle $= \frac{1}{2} \times b \times h$

$= \frac{1}{2} \times \ldots\ldots \times \ldots\ldots$

$= \ldots\ldots\ldots$ cm²

Area of rectangle = length × 6

$\ldots\ldots\ldots$ = length × 6

length = $\ldots\ldots\ldots \div 6$

= $\ldots\ldots\ldots\ldots$ cm

2. Six identical rectangles are used to make this larger rectangle.

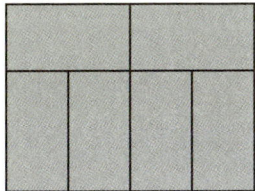

The perimeter of the larger rectangle is 63 cm.
Work out the area of one of the smaller rectangles. **(4 marks)**

$\ldots\ldots\ldots\ldots$ cm²

Links to:
Pages 79–81

Start by working out the area of the triangle. It is a right-angled triangle so you know the base and the vertical height.

You know that the area of the rectangle is the **same**. Use this to work out the length of the rectangle.

Look at the diagram to work out the relationship between the length and width of each small rectangle.

Problem solved!

Write the **width** of one small rectangle as *x* then work out the perimeter of the larger rectangle in terms of *x*.

Top exam tip!

Write out the formula you are using before you substitute any values.

Workout 20

21 3-D shapes

Warm up

 You need to be able to name these 3D shapes:
- cube
- cuboid
- cone
- pyramid

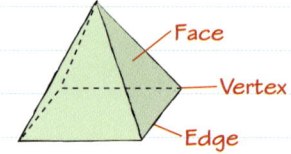

 The **volume** of a 3D shape is how much space it takes up.

 A **prism** has a constant cross-section.

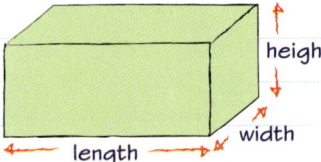

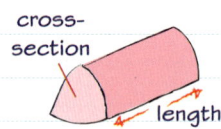

Volume = Length × Width × Height

Volume = Area of cross-section × Length

 To find the **surface area** of a 3D shape, add up the areas of all its faces.

Reps

Fill in the missing values.

a

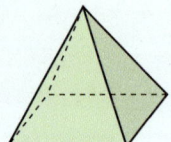

Faces = 5
Edges = ...
Vertices = ...

b

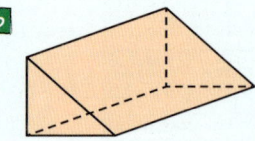

Faces = ...
Edges = ...
Vertices = ...

c

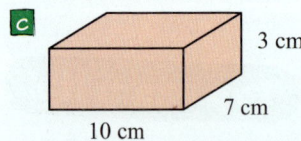

Volume = 210 cm³
Surface area = ... cm²

d

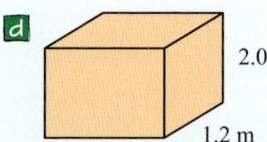

Volume = ... m³
Surface area = ... m²

GCSE Maths: Bootcamp

Exam practice

1. The total surface area of a cube is 150 cm². Work out the volume of the cube. **(4 marks)**

Area of each face = 150 ÷ ....

= .... cm²

Length of each side = $\sqrt{\ldots\ldots\ldots}$

= .... cm

Volume = ... × .... × ....

= ....

.... cm³

Links to:
Pages
82–84,
107–108

A cube has identical square faces. Divide 150 by the number of faces to work out the area of each face.

2. Here is a prism. The cross-section of the prism is in the shape of a trapezium.

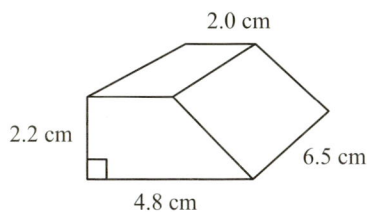

2.0 cm
2.2 cm
6.5 cm
4.8 cm

Work out the volume of the prism. **(4 marks)**

Start by working out the area of the cross-section. You need to use the formula for the area of a trapezium:

Area = $\frac{1}{2} \times (a + b) \times h$

A prism has a **constant** cross-section so the top of the front face is also 2.0 cm.

.... cm³

Top exam tip!

Write words with your working to show what you are working out at each stage.

22 Circles and cylinders

Warm up

- π is a number. Use π = 3.142 or the π on your calculator.
- Learn the names of the parts of a circle.
- Learn these circle formulae:
  1. Diameter = 2 × radius
  2. Area = πr^2
  3. Circumference = $2\pi r$
- A **cylinder** is a prism and so it has a constant circular cross-section.
  Volume of cylinder = $\pi r^2 h$
- If you need to use the formulae for the surface area or volume of a sphere or cone, they will be **given with the question**.

Reps

1. Work out the area and circumference of each circle to the nearest whole number.

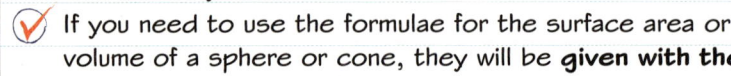

	a (7 cm)	b (3 cm)	c (5 m)	d (12 m)
Area	154 cm²	……… cm²	……… m²	……… m²
Circumference	……… cm	……… cm	……… m	……… m

2. Work out the volume of each cylinder to the nearest whole number.

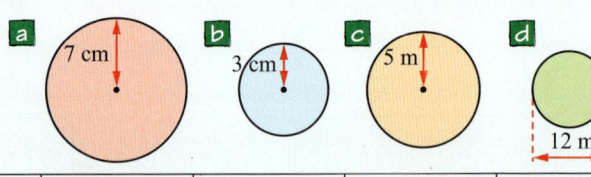
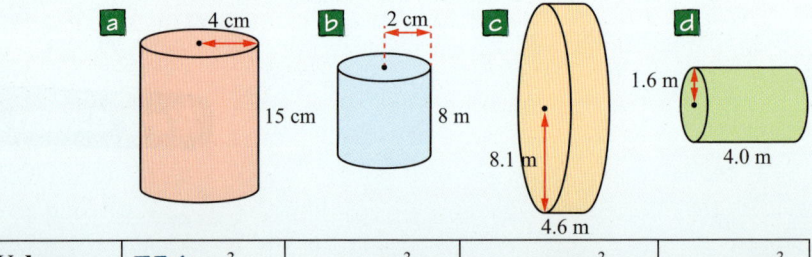

	a	b	c	d
Volume	754 cm³	……… m³	……… cm³	……… m³

GCSE Maths: Bootcamp

Exam practice

1. The diagram shows a semicircle with a diameter of 24 cm.

   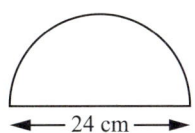

   (a) Work out the area of the semicircle. **(3 marks)**

   Guided

   Radius = 24 ÷ .... = ...

   Area of whole circle = πr^2 = $\pi \times$ ....^{2}

   = ... cm^2

   Area of semicircle = ... ÷ 2

   = ... cm^2

   (b) Work out the perimeter of the semicircle. **(3 marks)**

   .... cm

2. The diagram shows part of a roundabout.

   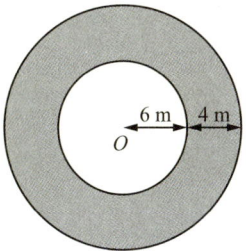

   The shaded area needs to be planted with grass seed. Each packet of seed covers 12 m^2. How many packets of grass seed will be needed? You must show your working.
   (5 marks)

Links to: Pages 103–106

Problem solved!

The formulae for area and circumference of a circle use the **radius**. You have been given the diameter so you need to divide by 2 to get the radius.

The perimeter is the length of half a circumference plus the length of one diameter.

Subtract the area of the small circle from the area of the large circle to find the shaded area.

You need a **whole number** of packets.

Top exam tip!

Your calculator might give answers in terms of π. Use the S⇔D key to convert them to decimal numbers.

Workout 22

23 Transformations

Warm up

 A **translation** is a sliding movement.

 You **reflect** a shape in a mirror line.

 A **rotation** must have a centre.

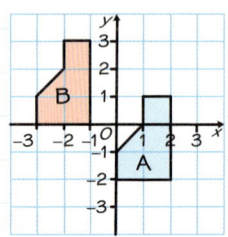

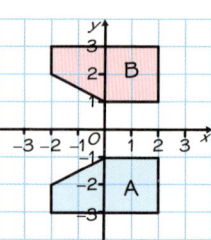

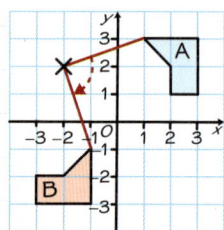

Translation of **A → B** by the vector $\begin{pmatrix} -3 \\ 2 \end{pmatrix}$

Reflection of **A → B** in the x-axis

Rotation of **A → B** 90° clockwise about centre of rotation (−2, 2)

 Enlargements make a shape bigger or smaller. The **scale factor**, k, tells you how much bigger or smaller the shape will be.

① $k > 1$: shape gets **larger** ② $0 < k < 1$: shape gets **smaller**

Reps

① On the grid, transform **T** by

A: translation by vector $\begin{pmatrix} 4 \\ -3 \end{pmatrix}$

B: rotation 90° clockwise about O

C: enlargement centre O with scale factor 2

D: translation by vector $\begin{pmatrix} 0 \\ 5 \end{pmatrix}$

E: reflection in line $x = 4$

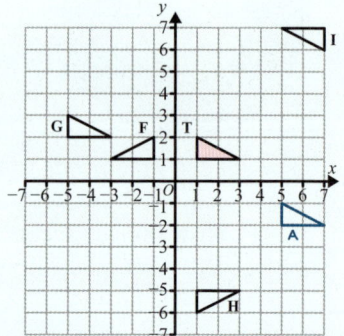

② Describe the transformation from T to

F: reflection in the y-axis **H**: ....

G: .... **I**: ....

GCSE Maths: Bootcamp

Exam practice

1.

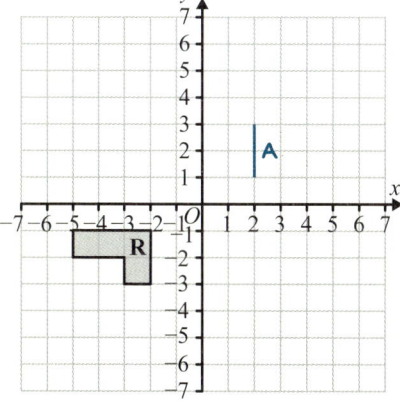

(a) Rotate shape **R** 180° about the origin. Label the new shape **A**. **(1 mark)**

(b) Translate shape **R** by the vector $\begin{pmatrix} -1 \\ 4 \end{pmatrix}$. Label the new shape **B**. **(1 mark)**

2.

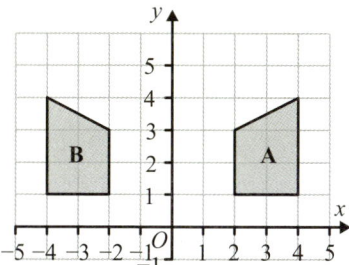

Describe fully the single transformation that maps shape **A** onto shape **B**. **(2 marks)**

....

....

> You can use tracing paper in your exam. Check a rotation by tracing the shape, then placing your pencil point on the centre of rotation. When you rotate the tracing paper your tracing should line up with your image.

> Write down the **name** of the transformation and:
> - the vector for a translation
> - the mirror line for a reflection
> - the centre and angle for a rotation
> - the centre and scale factor for an enlargement

Top exam tip!
Make sure you can identify and name the x-axis and the y-axis on a coordinate grid.

Workout 23

24 Pythagoras and trigonometry

Warm up

✓ The rules on this page apply to right-angled triangles.

✓ Learn **Pythagoras' theorem**:
$a^2 + b^2 = c^2$

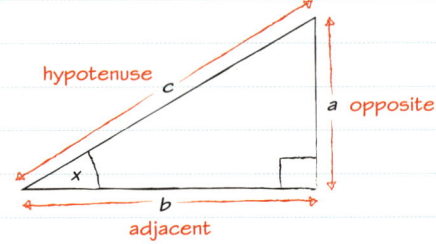

✓ Use **SOH CAH TOA** to remember the rules for sin, cos and tan:

① $\sin x = \dfrac{\text{opp}}{\text{hyp}}$ ② $\cos x = \dfrac{\text{adj}}{\text{hyp}}$ ③ $\tan x = \dfrac{\text{opp}}{\text{adj}}$

Reps

1 Find the lengths of the missing sides in these triangles to 1 decimal place.

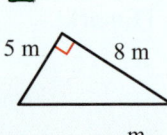 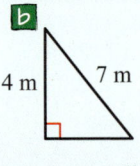 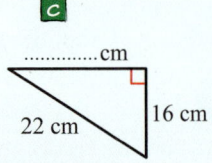

2 Find the sizes of the missing angles to the nearest degree.

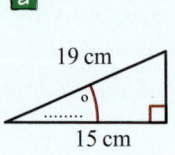 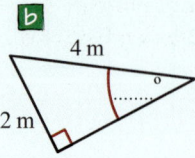 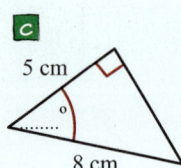

3 Find the lengths of the missing sides to 1 decimal place.

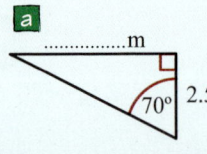 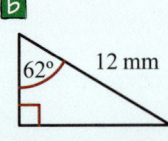 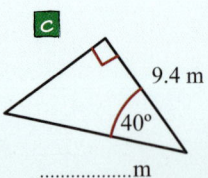

GCSE Maths: Bootcamp

Exam practice

1. ABC is a right-angled triangle.

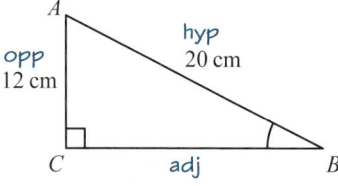

Work out the size of angle ABC. Give your answer to 1 decimal place. **(2 marks)**

Label the sides of the triangle in relation to the angle you are trying to find. You know the opposite and hypotenuse, so use
$$\sin x = \frac{opp}{hyp}$$

.......................°

Once you know $\sin x$, use the $\sin^{-1}$ function on your calculator to find x.

2. Here is a triangular prism.

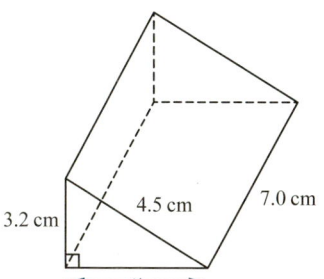

Work out the volume of the prism. Give your answer correct to 1 decimal place. **(5 marks)**

$x^2 + 3.2^2 = 4.5^2$

$x^2 = $ .... − ....

  $= $ ....

$x = $ .... cm

Area of cross-section $= \frac{1}{2} \times b \times h$

  $= $ ....

  $= $ .... cm^2

Volume of prism $= $ .... × ....

  $= $ .... cm^3

Problem solved!

*The formula for the area of a triangle uses base and vertical height. You need to use **Pythagoras' theorem** here to find the length of the base before you can calculate the area.*

Top exam tip!

Check that any lengths or angles make sense. The diagrams aren't to scale so you can't measure, but the values should look about right.

Links to: Pages 90–94

25 Bearings and constructions

Warm up

✓ Bearings are measured clockwise from north. They are written with **three figures**.

The bearing of B from A is 075°.

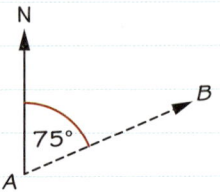

✓ You need to be able to accurately construct:

1 a perpendicular bisector

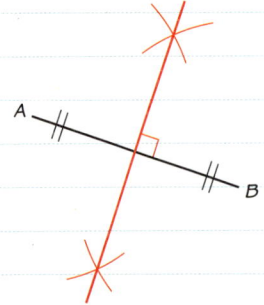

2 the bisector of an angle

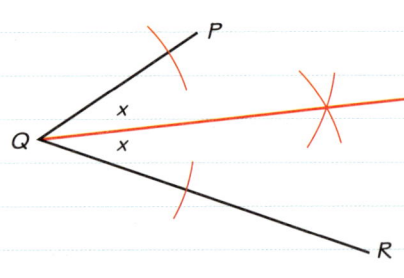

✓ To construct a triangle with given side lengths, draw one side with a ruler. Then set your compasses to the other side lengths and draw arcs with the points at each end of your line.

Reps

1 Construct an equilateral triangle with sides of length 4 cm. Label a 60° angle on your triangle.

4 cm

2 Bisect this angle using a ruler and compasses.

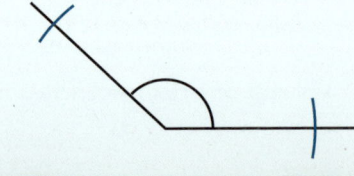

GCSE Maths: Bootcamp

Exam practice

  1. Using a ruler and a pair of compasses, accurately construct a perpendicular to this straight line that passes through the point *P*. **(3 marks)**

Guided

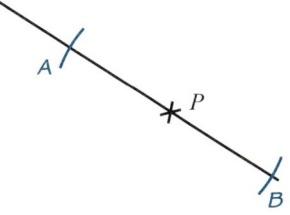

Perpendicular means at right angles to.

Start by putting your compasses point on *P*, and making two marks on the line an equal distance from *P*. These are marked A and B in the diagram. Then construct the perpendicular bisector of the line segment AB.

 2. The diagram shows two villages on a map.

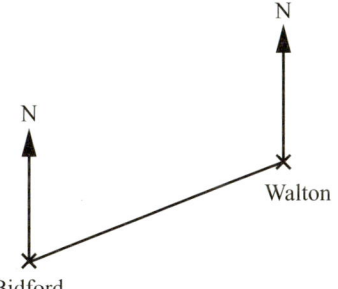

(a) Find the bearing of Bidford from Walton. **(1 mark)**

..............°

(b) Martin writes down the bearing of Walton from Bidford as 81°. What mistake has Martin made? **(1 mark)**

....

Measure the angle with a protractor. The bearing is **from Walton** so put the centre of your protractor on Walton and measure the clockwise angle from north.

Top exam tip!
If you are doing accurate constructions in your exam, don't rub out any of your compasses marks.

Links to: Pages 99, 100, 102

26 Similar and congruent

Warm up

✓ **Similar shapes** are an enlargement of one another. They have equal angles, and corresponding sides are in the same ratio.

✓ You can use ratios to work out missing sides in similar shapes.

$$\frac{EF}{AB} = \frac{6}{3} = 2$$

So EH = 2 × AD = 2 × 7 = 14 cm

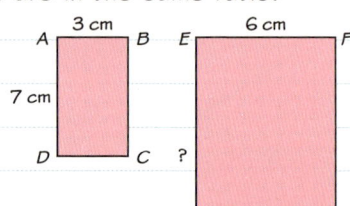

✓ **Congruent** shapes are exactly the same shape and size. To show that two triangles are congruent, you need to show **one** of these conditions:

1. SSS (three sides equal)
2. AAS (two angles and a corresponding side equal)
3. SAS (two sides equal and included angle equal)
4. RHS (right angle, hypotenuse and one side equal)

Reps

1. Find the missing lengths in each pair of similar shapes.

   a) 4 cm, 3 cm, ...cm, 12 cm, 9 cm, 21 cm

   b) 1.5 cm, 2.0 cm, 1.8 cm, ...cm

   c) ....m, 8 m, 20 m, 8.1 m, 3 m, ...m

2. Write down the condition that shows that each pair of triangles is congruent.

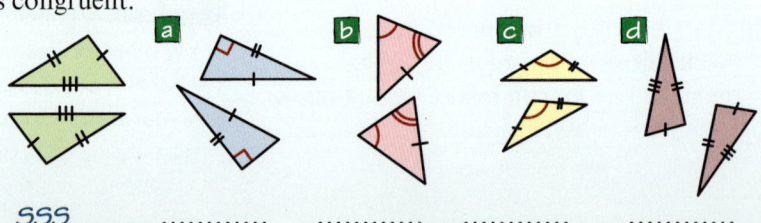

SSS   ....

GCSE Maths: Bootcamp

Exam practice

1. Triangle ABC is mathematically similar to triangle PQR.

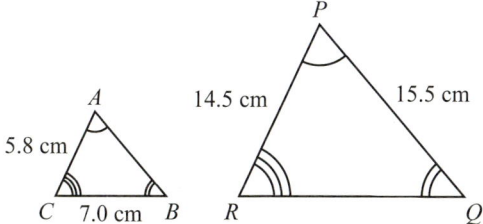

(a) Work out the length of QR. **(2 marks)**

.... cm

(b) Work out the length of AB. **(2 marks)**

.... cm

2. Show that these two triangles are mathematically similar.

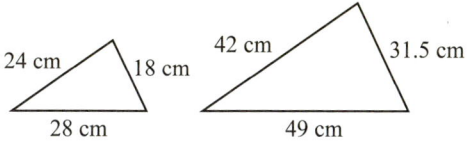

(3 marks)

Guided

$\dfrac{31.5}{18} = $ ....

$\dfrac{42}{\text{..............}} = $ ....

$\dfrac{\text{..............}}{\text{..............}} = $ ....

Corresponding sides in same ....

so the two triangles are ....

The markings show you which angles and sides correspond. You know that corresponding sides are in the same ratio.

Use side PR and side AC to work out the ratio. Then multiply or divide to find the missing lengths.

Problem solved!

To **show** that two triangles are similar you need to show one of these:
- corresponding sides are in the same ratio
- corresponding angles are equal
- two sides are in the same ratio and the angle between them is equal.

Top exam tip!

In a 'Show that ...' question the working **is** the answer. Make sure you write neatly so the examiner can read everything easily.

Workout 26

27 Graphs and charts

Warm up

✓ You need to be able to represent and interpret data on a:
- two-way table
- pie chart
- pictogram
- bar chart
- stem-and-leaf diagram
- line graph
- scatter graph

✓ **Frequency** is the number of times something occurs. You can use a **tally** to represent a frequency.

$\cancel{||||}$ = 5

Key: ◇ represents 4 people

✓ A **pictogram** is like a tally chart except you use a key instead of a tally.

✓ You can use a **scatter graph** or **scatter diagram** to show **correlation** and predict values using a **line of best fit**.

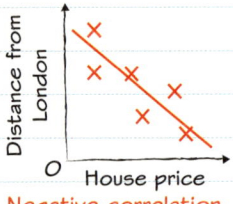
Negative correlation

No correlation

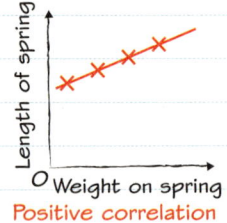
Positive correlation

Reps

1. The scatter graph shows the hourly cost of parking at 11 different car parks, and their distance from the town centre.

   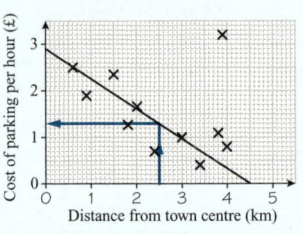

   a. One point is an outlier. Circle this point.
   b. Write down the type of correlation.

   ....

2. Use the line of best fit to estimate the hourly cost of parking at a car park that is

   2.5 km from the town centre   £1.30
   a. 1.2 km from the town centre   £...............
   b. 4 km from the town centre   £...............

GCSE Maths: Bootcamp

Exam practice

 1. This pictogram shows the number of cars sold last month by two different sales people.

| Emma | ① ① ① ① ① (|
| Takeshi | ① ① ① ① |

Key: ① represents **3 cars**

> Look at Emma's total and compare it to the key. Write your answer in words.

Write down one thing that is wrong with this pictogram. **(1 mark)**

....
....

> A pie chart shows frequencies as **proportions** of a **circle**.

 2. A group of people were asked what their favourite food to buy at the cinema was. The table shows their answers.

Food	Frequency	Angle
Sweets	9	9 × ......° = ...°
Popcorn	20	20 × ......° = ...°
Nachos	7	7 × ......° = ...°

> Divide 360° by the **total frequency** to work out the angle that represents 1 person on the pie chart. Then multiply each frequency by this angle.

Draw an accurate pie chart for this information.

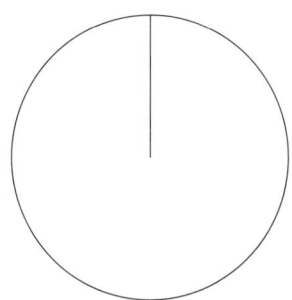

(3 marks)

> Use a ruler and a protractor, and try to be accurate to the nearest degree.

Total frequency = ... = ...

Angle for 1 person = 360° ÷ .... = ...°

Top exam tip!

Be neat and accurate when you are drawing graphs and charts. Use a **sharp** pencil!

Workout 27

28 Averages and range

Warm up

- The **mean, median** and **mode** are three different types of average.
- Mean = $\dfrac{\text{sum of data values}}{\text{number of data values}}$
- Mode = most commonly occurring value
- Median = middle value when the data values are written in order
- If data is given in a **frequency table** you need to look at the frequency, f, and the data value (or midpoint), x in each row:
  Mean = $\dfrac{\text{total of } f \times x \text{ column}}{\text{total frequency}}$
- **Range** is a measure of how spread out the data is:
  Range = largest value − smallest value

Reps

1 For each set of data values, find the mean, the median and the range.

    3 8 5 11 3   Mean = **6**   Median = **5**   Range = **8**

a 1.4 2.0 2.1 3.5   Mean = ...   Median = ...   Range = ...

b 2 2 3 4 8 8   Mean = ...   Median = ...   Range = ...

c 2 7 8 5 5   Mean = ...   Median = ...   Range = ...

d 10 15 22 13   Mean = ...   Median = ...   Range = ...

2 This frequency table shows the heights of some plants. Complete the table and find the mean and the class interval that contains the median.

Height, h (cm)	Frequency, f	Midpoint, x	$f \times x$
$0 \leqslant h < 10$	36	5	36 × 5 = 180
$10 \leqslant h < 20$	40		
$20 \leqslant h < 30$	24		
Totals			

Mean = ... cm   Class interval containing median = ...

GCSE Maths: Bootcamp

Exam practice

1. The frequency table shows the number of trips abroad taken by each member of a class in the last year.

Guided

Number of trips	Frequency	f × x
0	8	8 × 0 = 0
1	10	
2	7	
3	5	
4	1	
Total		

Add a column for frequency × number of trips, and a row for the totals.

(a) Work out the mean number of trips. **(3 marks)**

Check that your answers make sense. Everyone in the class took between 0 and 4 trips, so the mean must be between 0 and 4.

....

(b) What was the median number of trips? **(2 marks)**

If you wrote the data values in order of size, the first 8 values would be 0 and the next 10 would be 1.

....

2. The mean of the following five numbers is 12.6

18   7 x 16 x

Find the value of x. **(4 marks)**

Problem solved!

Don't just guess numbers. You need to find a strategy. Work out the **sum** of the data values first.

$x =$ ....

Top exam tip!

You can use this formula to solve some problems involving the mean:

mean × number of data values = sum of data values

Links to: Pages 120–122

29 Probability

Warm up

✓ Probabilities are numbers between 0 and 1. They are usually written as fractions or decimals.

✓ For equally likely outcomes:

$$\text{Probability} = \frac{\text{number of successful outcomes}}{\text{total number of possible outcomes}}$$

✓ P(event does not happen) = 1 − P(event happens)

✓ You can use a **tree diagram** to show independent events:
- multiply along the branches
- add up the outcomes

P(Blue then green) = $\frac{7}{8} \times \frac{1}{8} = \frac{7}{64}$

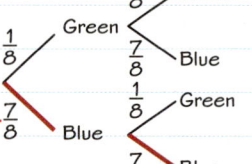

Reps

1 Draw a line to match each word to the correct place on the probability scale.

Even chance   Likely   Impossible   Certain   Unlikely

|---0---|---0.5---|---1---|

1 A fair six-sided dice is thrown. Find the probability of getting

a 1 — $\frac{1}{6}$

a. an even number ………
b. a square number ………
c. a number less than 6 ………
d. a number more than 7 ………

2 A fair coin is tossed three times. Find the probability of getting

three heads — $\frac{1}{8}$

a. three tails ………
b. tails on the last toss ………
c. heads on the first toss ………
d. tails on the first two tosses ………

GCSE Maths: Bootcamp

Exam practice

Links to:
Pages 128–130, 133

1. A bag contains 10 counters. They are:
   3 black squares   2 white squares
   1 black circle   4 white circles
   Soujit takes a counter at random.
   (a) Show that the probability of taking a white counter is $\frac{3}{5}$.   **(2 marks)**

   > Write down the number of successful outcomes, and the total number of outcomes. Then write the probability as a fraction and simplify it to $\frac{3}{5}$.

   Soujit returns the counter to the bag and picks another counter at random. He does this experiment 50 times.
   (b) Work out an estimate for the number of times he picks a white counter.   **(2 marks)**

   > To find the **expected** number of times an event occurs, multiply the probability by the number of trials.

   ....

2. A spinner can land on red or green or blue. The table shows the probabilities of landing on red or green.

Colour	Red	Green	Blue
Probability	0.2	0.5	....

   The spinner is spun once.
   (a) Work out the probability of landing on blue.   **(1 mark)**

   > The sum of all the possible outcomes of an event is 1.

   ....

   The spinner is spun twice.
   (b) Work out the probability of landing on the same colour twice.   **(3 marks)**

   > There are three ways of landing on the same colour:
   > - red, red
   > - green, green
   > - blue, blue

   P(red, red) = 0.2 × 0.2 = 0.04
   P(green, green) = ... × .... = ...
   P(blue, blue) = ... × .... = ...
   P(same colour) = 0.04 + ... + ...
                  = ...

   ### Top exam tip!
   You can give probabilities as fractions or decimals in your exam.

30 Venn diagrams

Warm up

✓ Venn diagrams can show frequencies or outcomes:

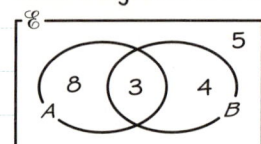

There are $8 + 3 = 11$ outcomes in event A.
There are $8 + 3 + 4 + 5 = 20$ outcomes in the **whole sample space**. So
$P(A) = \frac{11}{20}$

✓ The event $A \cap B$ means A **and** B (or A **intersection** B)

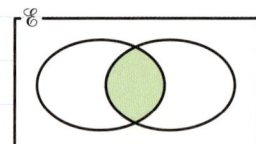

✓ The event $A \cup B$ means A **or** B (or A **union** B)

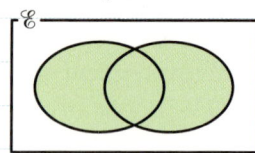

✓ You can also use a **frequency** tree to show all the possible outcomes of two events. Each frequency equals the sum of its branches.

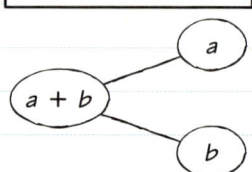

Reps

Shade the events shown, and write down the probability of each event.

Not A

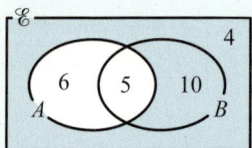

$P(\text{Not } A) = \frac{14}{25}$

a B

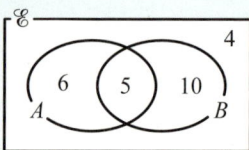

$P(B) = \ldots\ldots\ldots$

b $A \cap B$

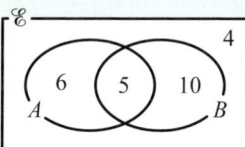

$P(A \cap B) = \ldots\ldots\ldots$

c Not B

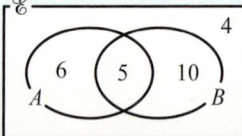

$P(\text{Not } B) = \ldots\ldots\ldots$

d $A \cup B$

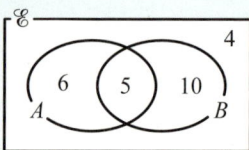

$P(A \cup B) = \ldots\ldots\ldots$

e Neither A nor B

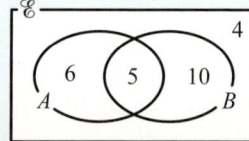

$P(\text{Neither } A \text{ nor } B) = \ldots\ldots\ldots$

GCSE Maths: Bootcamp

Exam practice

1. There are 650 students at a college.
429 of them have passed their driving test.
185 males have passed their driving test.
290 students are male.
Use this information to complete the frequency tree.

Guided

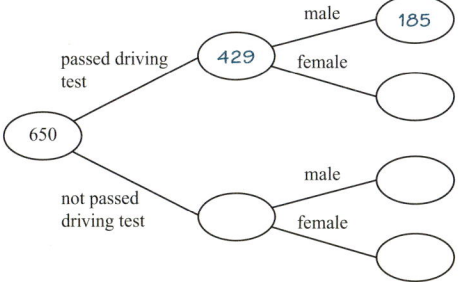

> You know there are 290 male students so work out 290 − 185 to complete the third box on the right.

> Use the rule for frequency trees given opposite to find the missing values.

> Check that the four boxes on the right add up to 650.

(3 marks)

2. $\mathcal{E}$ = {prime numbers less than 30}
A = {2, 7, 11, 23}
B = {3, 5, 7}

(a) Complete the Venn diagram to show this information.

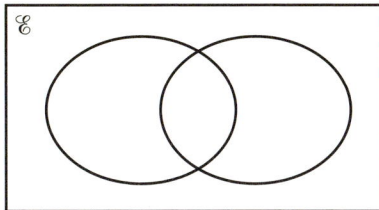

> $\mathcal{E}$ represents the **universal set**. Every member of the universal set should appear **exactly once** on the Venn diagram.

A number is chosen at random from the universal set $\mathcal{E}$ (4 marks)

(b) What is the probability that it is in the set $A \cup B$? (2 marks)

> In this case the numbers on the Venn diagram will represent the outcomes themselves, not the total number of possible outcomes.

....

Workout 30

Answers

1 Number crunch

Reps

1 In the number 3215.49 write down the value of
- **a** the 1 — 1 ten
- **b** the 4 — 4 tenths
- **c** the 5 — 5 units
- **d** the 2 — 2 hundreds

2 Write in order, smallest first.
- **a** 40 30 9 — 9 30 40
- **b** −3 −8 0 — −8 −3 0
- **c** 5 −10 7 — −10 5 7
- **d** 21 −3 −5 — −5 −3 21

3 Work out mentally
- **a** −3 × 20 — −60
- **b** 30 × 8 — 240
- **c** 120 ÷ 4 — 30
- **d** 90 ÷ 6 — 15

4 Use a written method to work out
- **a** 137 × 21 — 2877
- **b** 2275 − 188 — 2087
- **c** 1617 ÷ 7 — 231
- **d** 452 + 1296 — 1748

Exam practice

1. Here are four different digits.

   7   5   1   9

(a) Write one digit in each box to give the sum with the largest possible answer. One has been done for you. You may only use each digit once.

  −

(b) Use three of the digits above to make the smallest possible positive number.

.157.

2. Angela buys
  6 exercise books costing £1.20 each
  1 pencil sharpener costing 80p
  3 ink cartridges

She pays with a £10 note and gets 65p change.

Work out the cost of one ink cartridge. You must show all your working.

6 × 120 = 720
1 × 80 = 80
So the exercise books and pencil sharpener cost 800p (or £8).
1000 − 65 = 935
935 − 800 = 135

```
      4 5
   3 |1 3 ¹5
```

Each ink cartridge cost 45p.

Workout 1 answers

Answers

2 Fractions and decimals

Reps

1 Work out
a) 12.7 + 9.2 — 21.9
b) 20.3 − 5.9 — 14.4
c) 3.2 × 6 — 19.2
d) 12.5 ÷ 5 — 2.5

2 Fill in the equivalent fractions.
a) $\frac{1}{5} = \frac{\boxed{3}}{15}$
b) $\frac{\boxed{3}}{4} = \frac{9}{12}$
c) $\frac{2}{5} = \frac{10}{\boxed{25}}$
d) $\frac{15}{\boxed{20}} = \frac{3}{4}$

3 Find
a) $\frac{1}{2}$ of 200 ml — 100 ml
b) $\frac{2}{3}$ of 90 km — 60 km
c) $\frac{3}{5}$ of 60 kg — 36 kg
d) $\frac{9}{10}$ of 5 cm — 4.5 cm

4 Work out
a) $\frac{1}{2} + \frac{1}{4}$ — $\frac{3}{4}$
b) $\frac{1}{2} \times \frac{3}{5}$ — $\frac{3}{10}$
c) $4\frac{2}{3} - 2\frac{1}{4}$ — $2\frac{5}{12}$
d) $\frac{1}{6} \div \frac{3}{4}$ — $\frac{2}{9}$

Exam practice

1. Alice thinks of a number.
$\frac{1}{4}$ of Alice's number is 10
Work out $\frac{2}{5}$ of Alice's number.

10 × 4 = 40 = Alice's number
40 ÷ 5 = 8
8 × 2 = 16

2. Work out 24.7 × 5.8

```
      2 4 7
×       5 8
    -------
      1 9 7 6
        3 5
    1 2 3 5 0
      2 3
    -------
    1 4 3 2 6
      1 1
```

2 decimal places

143.26

3. Work out $1\frac{1}{4} \times 2\frac{3}{5}$
Give your answer as a mixed number.

$1\frac{1}{4} \times 2\frac{3}{5} = \frac{5}{4} \times \frac{13}{5}$
$= \frac{13}{4}$
$= 3\frac{1}{4}$

Workout 2 answers

Answers

3 Powers and roots

Reps

1 Work out
- a) 11^2 — 121
- b) $(3+1)^0$ — 1
- c) $\sqrt{225}$ — 15
- d) $5^2 - 2 \times 4$ — 17

2 Write as a single power of 5
- a) $5^2 \times 5^7$ — 5^9
- b) $(5^3)^2$ — 5^6
- c) $\frac{1}{125}$ — 5^{-3}
- d) 25^5 — 5^{10}

3 Write in standard form
- a) 29 000 — 2.9×10^4
- b) 0.05 — 5×10^{-2}
- c) 9 010 000 — 9.01×10^6
- d) 0.000 06 — 6×10^{-5}

4 Write as an ordinary number
- a) 6.9×10^{-1} — 0.69
- b) 8×10^4 — 80 000
- c) 2.03×10^2 — 203
- d) 5.5×10^{-3} — 0.0055

Exam practice

1. Work out the value of
(a) $(7.1 - 2.5)^2 - 4.35$

$7.1 - 2.5 = 4.6$
$4.6^2 = 21.16$
$21.16 - 4.35 = 16.81$

(b) 3^{-2}

$3^{-2} = \frac{1}{3^2} = \frac{1}{9}$

$\frac{1}{9}$

2. Work out $(6.5 \times 10^8) \times (2 \times 10^{-13})$
Give your answer as an ordinary number.

$6.5 \times 2 \times 10^8 \times 10^{-13}$
$= 13 \times 10^{-5}$
$= 1.3 \times 10^{-4}$

0.00013

3. Work out $\frac{0.05 \times 0.0007}{0.01}$
Give your answer in standard form.

$0.05 \times 0.0007 = 5 \times 10^{-2} \times 7 \times 10^{-4}$
$= 5 \times 7 \times 10^{-2 + {-4}}$
$= 35 \times 10^{-6}$
$= 3.5 \times 10^{-5}$

$3.5 \times 10^{-5} \times 100 = 3.5 \times 10^{-5 + 2}$
$= 3.5 \times 10^{-3}$

Workout 3 answers

4 Rounding, estimation and error

Reps

1 Round 7256.5 to the nearest
- **a** ten — 7260
- **b** whole number — 7257
- **c** thousand — 7000

2 Round to 1 significant figure.
- **a** 0.251 — 0.3
- **b** 8.70 — 9
- **c** 345 — 300
- **d** 0.00372 — 0.004

3 Estimate the answer by rounding each number.
- **a** 5.5×8.9 — 54
- **b** $29.3 \div 4.5$ — 6
- **c** 7.75^2 — 64
- **d** 391×0.470 — 200

4 Write the missing number in each error interval.
- **a** $8500 \leq x < 9500$
- **b** $0.65 \leq x < 0.75$
- **c** $10.5 \leq x < 11.5$
- **d** $2.95 \leq x < 3.05$

Exam practice

1. Amir wants to buy 22 photo frames. Each photo frame costs £3.35
Amir does the calculation $20 \times 3 = 60$ to estimate the cost of the 22 photo frames.
Explain how Amir's calculation shows that the actual cost will be more than £60.

Both values have been rounded down. So the actual answer will be more than £60.

2. Work out an estimate for
$$\frac{221 \times 5.2}{0.185}$$

$$\frac{221 \times 5.2}{0.185} \approx \frac{200 \times 5}{0.2}$$
$$= \frac{1000}{0.2}$$
$$= \frac{10000}{2}$$
$$= 5000$$

3. A number, n, is rounded to 1 decimal place. The result is 10.5
Write down the error interval for n.

$$10.45 \leq n < 10.55$$

Workout 4 answers

Answers

5 Factors, multiples and primes

Reps

1 11, 12, 13, 14, 15, 16, 17, 18
From the list write down

a a factor of 30   15

b a multiple of 9   18

c two multiples of 4   12, 16

d any prime numbers   11, 13, 17

2 Circle any prime factors of the given number in each list.

a 28   4   ⑦   14   28

b 39   1   ③   9   ⑬

c 45   ③   ⑤   9   15

d 100   ②   ⑤   10   50

3 a Fill in the Venn diagram to show the factors of 20 and the factors of 30.
b Write down the highest common factor of 20 and 30   10

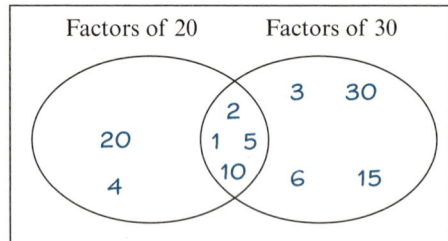

Exam practice

1. Becca says
'There are twice as many prime numbers between 10 and 20 as there are between 20 and 30.'
Is Becca correct? Show how you got your answer.

Prime numbers between 10 and 20:
11, 13, 17, 19

Prime numbers between 20 and 30:
23, 29

Conclusion:
4 is twice as many as 2, so Becca is correct.

2. (a) Write 96 as a product of its prime factors.

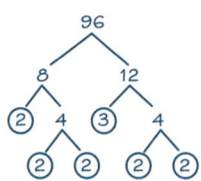

$96 = 2^5 \times 3$

(b) Find the highest common factor (HCF) of 96 and 30

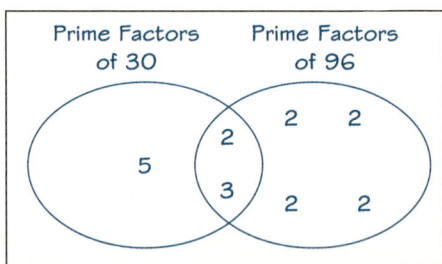

$2 \times 3 = 6$

......6..

6 Algebra essentials

Reps

1 Circle the pair of like terms in each list.

a 2p 3q (5r) 2pq (4r)

b (ab) 2a² 3b (2ab) ab²

c (2m²) m²n 5mn (m²) 3m

d 3xy (2x²y) xy² 2x (x²y)

2 Simplify by collecting like terms.

a $10x - 6x$ $4x$

b $4p + 2p - p$ $5p$

c $7m + n + 3n + m$ $8m + 4n$

d $4a - b + 2a - 5b$ $6a - 6b$

3 Use the index laws to simplify

a $a^4 \times a$ a^5

b $(c^2)^3$ c^6

c $\dfrac{x^{10}}{x^2}$ x^8

d $\dfrac{b^2 \times b^{10}}{b^3}$ b^6

4 Match the simplified expressions.

a $4x \times 2xy^2$ ———— $8x^2y^2$

b $2x^2y \times xy^2$ $2xy$

c $\dfrac{2x^2y}{x}$ $4x^2y^3$

d $x^2y \times 4y^2$ $2x^3y^3$

Exam practice

1. (a) Simplify $10x - 3x + x$

$8x$

(b) Simplify $n^2 + n^2 + n^2$

$3n^2$

(c) Simplify $4p - 5q - p + 6 - 2q$

$4p - p - 5q - 2q + 6$

$3p - 7q + 6$

(d) Simplify $\dfrac{3y + 5y}{2}$

$\dfrac{8y}{2}$

$4y$

2. $(3x + y)$ cm

$2y$ cm

Write an expression for the perimeter of this rectangle. Simplify your answer.

$(3x + y) + 2y + (3x + y) + 2y$
$= 3x + 3x + y + 2y + y + 2y$
$= 6x + 6y$

$(6x + 6y)$ cm

3. Simplify $(2ab^2)^3$

$2^3 \times a^3 \times (b^2)^3 = 8 \times a^3 \times b^6$

$8a^3b^6$

Workout 6 answers

Answers

7 Brackets and factorising

Reps

1 Expand
- a) $6(n+2)$ — $6n+12$
- b) $a(2a+b)$ — $2a^2+ab$
- c) $5x(2-x)$ — $10x-5x^2$
- d) $2p(3q+2p^2)$ — $6pq+4p^3$

2 Factorise fully
- a) $2m+6$ — $2(m+3)$
- b) $10a^2-2a$ — $2a(5a-1)$
- c) x^2+3x — $x(x+3)$
- d) $2x^3-4xy$ — $2x(x^2-2y)$

3 Expand and simplify
- a) $n(2+n)+3n$ — $5n+n^2$
- b) $5(p+1)-2(1-p)$ — $7p+3$
- c) $(y+1)(y-3)$ — y^2-2y-3
- d) $(e-2)(e-5)$ — $e^2-7e+10$

4 Factorise
- a) x^2+3x+2 — $(x+2)(x+1)$
- b) y^2-4y+3 — $(y-1)(y-3)$
- c) n^2+6n+9 — $(n+3)(n+3)$
- d) x^2-x-6 — $(x+2)(x-3)$

Exam practice

1. Expand and simplify
$5(2x-1)-5(x+3)$
$=10x-5-5x-15$
$=5x-20$

$5x-20$

2. Expand and simplify $(2x+1)(x+3)$.

	x	$+3$
$2x$	$2x^2$	$+6x$
$+1$	$+x$	$+3$

$2x^2+6x+x+3=2x^2+7x+3$

3. Factorise fully
(a) $4y^2+10y$
$=2(2y^2+5y)$
$=2y(2y+5)$

(b) $x^2+7x+10$
$5+2=7$
$5\times 2=10$

$x^2+7x+10=(x+2)(x+5)$

$(x+2)(x+5)$

Workout 7 answers

8 Equations and inequalities

Reps

1 Solve
- **a** $x - 12 = 3$ $x = 15$
- **b** $2x = 5$ $x = 2.5$
- **c** $x + 9 = 4$ $x = -5$
- **d** $\frac{x}{6} = 3.5$ $x = 21$

2 Solve
- **a** $10x - 10 = 60$ $x = 7$
- **b** $2x + 1 = 6x - 9$ $x = 2.5$
- **c** $8 - 8x = 20 - 2x$ $x = -2$
- **d** $2(x - 3) = 7$ $x = 6.5$

3 Write down all the integers that satisfy each inequality.
- **a** $3 < x < 7$ 4, 5, 6
- **b** $-5 \leqslant x < -3$ $-5, -4$
- **c** $0 \leqslant x \leqslant 3$ 0, 1, 2, 3
- **d** $10 < x < 15$ 11, 12, 13, 14

4 Solve each inequality:
- **a** $2x < 10$ $x < 5$
- **b** $x + 8 \geqslant 2$ $x \geqslant -6$
- **c** $3x - 2 \leqslant 10$ $x \leqslant 4$
- **d** $x + 1 \geqslant 2x + 5$ $x \leqslant -4$

Exam practice

1. $-1 \leqslant n < 4$
n is an integer. Write down all the possible values of n.

$-1, 0, 1, 2, 3$

2. Solve $\frac{2x + 1}{3} = x - 7$

$2x + 1 = 3x - 21$
$2x = 3x - 22$
$-x = -22$

$x = 22$

3. Find the area of this square.

(3x − 5) cm

(x + 2) cm

$3x - 5 = x + 2$
$3x = x + 7$
$2x = 7$
$x = 3.5$
Side length = 3.5
So area = $3.5^2 = 12.25$

12.25 cm^2

9 Formulae

Reps

1 Write 'expression', 'equation' or 'formula'.
a) $2y = 8$ — equation
b) $10x^2 - 1$ — expression
c) $p = 2q + 1$ — formula
d) $x = 2x - 5$ — equation

2 If $x = 2$ and $y = 5$, find the value of
a) $10y + 1$ — 51
b) $2y - x$ — 8
c) $15x - y^2$ — 5
d) $5x + xy$ — 20

3 Make Q the subject of each formula.
a) $P = Q + 50$ → $Q = P - 50$
b) $P = \dfrac{Q+1}{5}$ → $Q = 5P - 1$
c) $P = 10R - 5Q$ → $Q = \dfrac{10R - P}{5}$
d) $P = 2QR + 5$ → $Q = \dfrac{P - 5}{2R}$

Exam practice

1. | expression equation formula identity inequality term factor multiple |

Choose two words from the box to make a correct statement.

$2x$ is a <u>term</u> in the <u>expression</u> $2x - y$

3. $P = \sqrt{y + 10}$

(a) Work out the value of P when $y = 15$
$P = \sqrt{15 + 10}$
$= \sqrt{25} = 5$

$\underline{P = 5}$

(b) Make y the subject of the formula $P = \sqrt{y + 10}$
$P^2 = y + 10$
$y = P^2 - 10$

$\underline{y = P^2 - 10}$

2. This path is made up of 6 identical rectangular pavers of length x, and one paver of length 4. The total length of the path is L. All measurements are in metres.

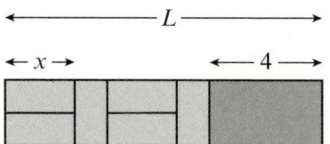

Find a formula for L in terms of x. Write your formula as simply as possible.

$L = x + \tfrac{1}{2}x + x + \tfrac{1}{2}x + 4$
$= 3x + 4$

$\underline{L = 3x + 4}$

10 Sequences

Reps

1 Find the next two terms in each sequence.

a) −1 4 9 14 19   24   29
b) 100 90 80 70   60   50
c) 1 2 3 5 8   13   21
d) 1 4 9 16 25   36   49

2 Write the rule to get from one term to the next.

a) 5 7 9 11 13   add 2
b) 10 15 20 25   add 5
c) 14 8 2 −4   subtract 6
d) 3 6 12 24 48   multiply by 2

3 Write the first three terms in these sequences with an nth term.

a) $3n + 10$ 13   16   19
b) $20 - 2n$ 18   16   14
c) n^3 1   8   27
d) $2n^2$ 2   8   18

4 Find the nth term of each arithmetic sequence.

a) 2 4 6 8 10 $2n$
b) 10 15 20 25 30 $5n + 5$
c) −1 5 11 17 23 $6n - 7$
d) 1 10 19 28 37 $9n - 8$

Exam practice

1. Here are the first six terms of an arithmetic sequence.
4   11   18   25   32   29
Find an expression, in terms of n, for the nth term of this sequence.

Common difference = 7
Multiples of 6 are 7, 14, 21, 28, …
nth term = $7n - 3$

2. The nth term in an arithmetic sequence is $6n - 1$
Is 103 a term in this sequence?
Show how you get your answer.

$6n - 1 = 103$
$6n = 104$
$n = 17.33…$
n is not an integer, so 103 is not a term in the sequence.

3. The rule to get from one term to the next term in a sequence is

> Add k then multiply by 2

The first term is 7 and the second term is 20
Find the third term in the sequence.

$2(7 + k) = 20$ (1st term)
$14 + 2k = 20$
$2k = 6$
$k = 3$
$20 + 3 = 23$
$23 \times 2 = 46$

Answers

11 Coordinates and lines

Reps

1 Write down the coordinates of each point.
- **a** Q = (1, 4)
- **b** R = (3, 0)
- **c** S = (2, –1)
- **d** T = (5, –2)

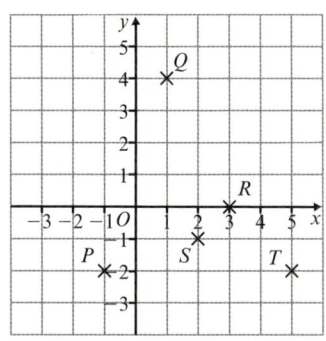

2 Match each line to the correct equation.

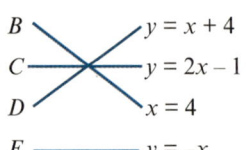

B — y = x + 4
C — y = 2x – 1
D — x = 4
E — y = –x

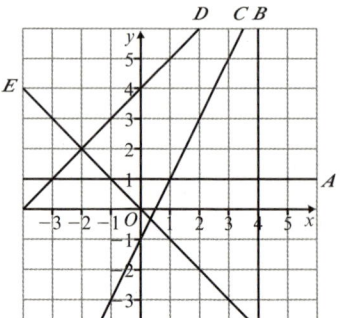

Exam practice

1. The diagram shows three identical squares.

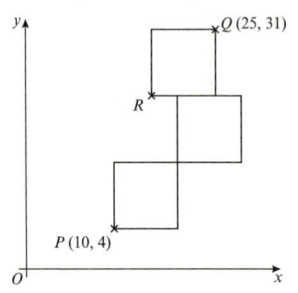

Work out the coordinates of point R.
31 – 4 = 27
27 ÷ 3 = 9
Each side is 9 units
25 – 9 = 16 and 31 – 9 = 22
(16, 22)

2. A straight line passes through the points (0, –2) and (3, 7).
Find an equation of the line.

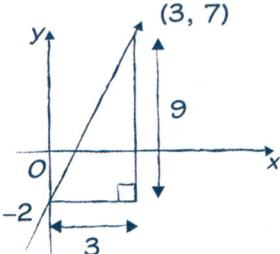

Gradient = $\frac{9}{3}$ = 3
y-intercept = –2
Equation is y = 3x – 2

Workout 11 answers

12 Real-life graphs

Reps

1 The diagram shows a travel graph for an orienteering competition.
Find the speed of the competitor in

a section B   0 km/h
b section C   6 km/h
c section D   2.75 km/h

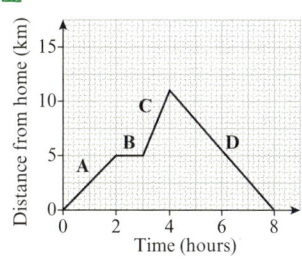

2 In which section was the competitor

a returning home   D
b moving fastest   C
c not moving   B

3 Write down the letter that describes each velocity–time graph.

A Decelerating   **B** Stationary   **C** Constant speed   **D** Accelerating

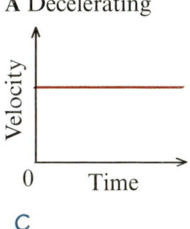   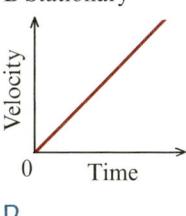   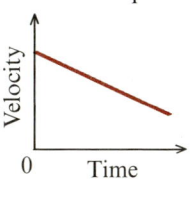 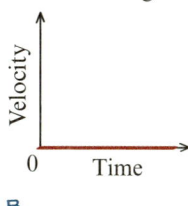

C   D   A   B

Exam practice

1. You can use this graph to convert between kilograms and pounds.

(a) Change 34 kg into lb.

                                    74 lb

1 tonne = 1000 kg

(b) Explain how you could use your answer to convert 3.4 tonnes into lb.

By multiplying the answer above by 100

Alice says that the graph shows that kilograms are directly proportional to pounds.

(c) Is Alice correct? Explain your answer.

Yes, because it is a straight line through the origin

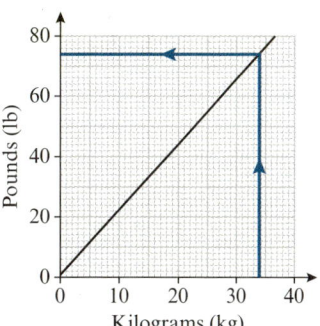

Answers

13 Curvy graphs

Reps

1 Write 'curvy' or 'straight' next to each equation to describe the graph.

a $y = x^2$ curvy
b $y = 10 - x$ straight
c $x = 5$ straight
d $y = x^3 + 2$ curvy

2 Write down the letter of the matching equation.

A $y = 3 - x$
B $y = 10 - x^2$
C $y = x^3 - x^2$
D $y = \frac{1}{2}x - 1$

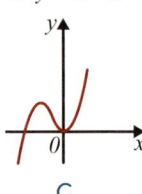
C

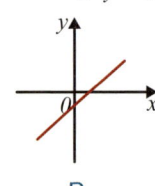
D

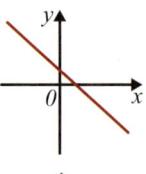
A

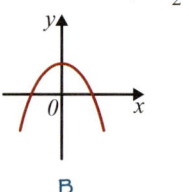
B

Exam practice

1. (a) On the grid, draw the graph of $y = x^2 + 2x - 1$
You can use the table of values to help you.

x	–3	–2	–1	0	1
y	2	–1	–2	–1	2

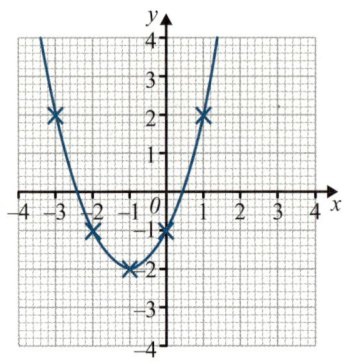

(b) Write down the coordinates of the turning point on the graph.

(–1, –2)

(c) Write down the solutions to $x^2 + 2x - 1 = 0$

x = –2.4 or 0.4

2. Steven has drawn part of a graph of $y = x - \frac{1}{10}x^3$

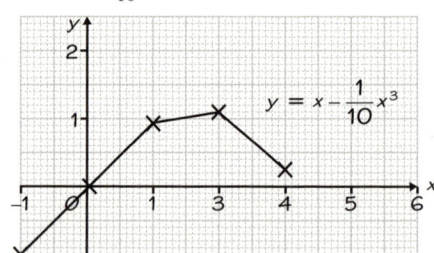

Write down two things that are wrong with Steven's graph.

The points are joined with straight lines rather than a smooth curve.

The horizontal axis is not numbered correctly.

Workout 13 answers

14 Tricky algebra

Answers

Reps

1 Assuming k is an integer, write odd or even for each expression.
- **a** $10k$ — even
- **b** $k(k + 1)$ — even
- **c** $4k + 5$ — odd
- **d** $k + (k + 3)$ — odd

2 Write down the answers to each factorised quadratic equation.
- **a** $(x - 4)(x - 3) = 0$ — $x = 4$ or 3
- **b** $(x + 2)(x + 2) = 0$ — $x = -2$
- **c** $(x + 1)(x - 7) = 0$ — $x = -1$ or 7
- **d** $(x + 4)(x - 2) = 0$ — $x = -4$ or 2

3 Multiply every term in each linear equation by 2
- **a** $x - 4y = 2$ — $2x - 8y = 4$
- **b** $3x + 5y = 7$ — $6x + 10y = 14$
- **c** $2x = 6y + 1$ — $4x = 12y + 2$
- **d** $y = 3 - x$ — $2y = 6 - 2x$

Exam practice

1. Solve $x^2 + 4x - 21 = 0$
$(x + 7)(x - 3) = 0$
When $x + 7 = 0$, $x = -7$
When $x - 3 = 0$, $x = 3$
Solution is $x = -7$ or $x = 3$

3. Solve the simultaneous equations
$x + y = 6$ ①
$2x - 4y = 3$ ②
$2 \times$ ①: $\quad 2x + 2y = 12$
$-$ ②: $\quad 2x - 4y = 3$
_____
$2x + 2y - (2x - 4y) = 6y$
$12 - 3 = 9$

So $6y = 9$
$y = 1.5$
Substitute into ①:
$x + 1.5 = 6$
$x = 4.5$

$x = \underline{4.5}$
$y = \underline{1.5}$

2. **(a)** Use algebra to show that the sum of two odd numbers is always an even number.
$(2n + 1) + (2m + 1) = 2n + 2m + 2$
$= 2(n + m + 1)$
$n + m + 1$ is an integer, so
$2(n + m + 1)$ must be an even number.
x and y are consecutive numbers.

(b) Explain why their sum will always be an odd number.

One must be odd and one must be even. Odd + even = odd.

Workout 14 answers

Answers

15 Percentages

Reps

1 Find

- **a** 20% of 600 g — 120 g
- **b** 5% of 80 km — 4 km
- **c** 75% of 2 kg — 1.5 kg
- **d** 43% of 7200 ml — 3096 ml

2 Write each amount as a percentage of £2500.

- **a** £1250 — 50%
- **b** £1000 — 40%
- **c** £300 — 12%
- **d** £1700 — 68%

3 Write the correct multiplier.

- **a** 50% increase — 1.5
- **b** 20% decrease — 0.8
- **c** 3% increase — 1.03
- **d** 42% decrease — 0.58

4 Increase each amount by 35%.

- **a** 50 g — 67.5 g
- **b** 1.8 m — 2.43 m
- **c** 90 kg — 121.5 kg
- **d** 1000 km — 1350 km

Exam practice

1. (a) Write $\frac{3}{5}$ as a percentage.

   60%

   (b) Write 0.85 as a percentage.

   85%

2. All the employees at a company receive a 5% pay rise.

   (a) Paula was paid £1800 per month **before** the pay rise. Work out her monthly pay after the pay rise.

   Multiplier for 5% increase = 1.05
   1800 × 1.05 = 1890

   £1890

   (b) Dhruv was paid £1470 **after** the pay rise. Work out his monthly pay before the pay rise.

   1470 ÷ 1.05 = 1400

   £1400

3. Jaden buys 20 bars of chocolate for a total of £7.95
   She sells all 20 bars for 60p each.
   Work out Jaden's percentage profit.
   Give your answer to 1 decimal place.

   Total selling price:
   20 × 0.6 = £12
   Profit:
   12 − 7.95 = £4.05
   Percentage profit:

   $\frac{4.05}{7.95} \times 100 = 50.943...\%$

   50.9%

Workout 15 answers

16 Ratio and proportion

Reps

1 Write these ratios in simplest form.

- **a** 5:10   1:2
- **b** 25:10   5:2
- **c** 2:10:12   1:5:6
- **d** 12:30:15   4:10:5

2 Divide £600 in the ratio

- **a** 1:3   £150 and £450
- **b** 5:1   £500 and £100
- **c** 5:7   £250 and £350
- **d** 1:9   £60 and £540

3 y is directly proportional to x.
When $y = 3$, $x = 10$ Find

- **a** y when $x = 5$ 1.5
- **b** x when $y = 15$ 50
- **c** y when $x = 100$ 30
- **d** y when $x = 8$ 2.4

4 12 kg of potatoes cost £9.12
Find the cost of

- **a** 1 kg   76p
- **b** 5 kg   £3.80
- **c** 15 kg   £11.40
- **d** 750 g   57p

Exam practice

1. A jar of biscuits contains only ginger nuts, chocolate digestives and plain digestives, in the ratio 6:5:9
Work out what percentage of the biscuits are ginger nuts.

$6 + 5 + 9 = 20$
$\frac{6}{20} = \frac{30}{100}$
             30%

2. Alison is 2 years younger than Christina. The sum of their ages is 30.
Find the ratio of Alison's age to Christina's age. Give your answer in its simplest form.

$a + (a + 2) = 30$
$2a + 2 = 30$
$2a = 28$
$a = 14$
Alison:Christina = 14:16
               = 7:8

3. A brand of cereal is sold in two different sized boxes

| Standard size (500 g): £1.50 |
| Family size (750 g): £2.10 |

Which box offers the better value? Give reasons for your answer.

Standard:
$150 \div 500 = 0.3$
0.3 pence per gram

Family:
$210 \div 750 = 0.28$
0.28 pence per gram

Family size is cheaper per gram so is better value.

Answers

17 Measuring and estimating

Reps

1 Convert
- **a** 65 cm into m — 0.65 m
- **b** 0.15 litres into ml — 150 ml
- **c** 2400 g into kg — 2.4 kg
- **d** 420 m into km — 0.42 km

2 Write each time in the 24-hour clock.
- **a** 2.15 pm — 14:15
- **b** 12.45 am — 00:45
- **c** 7.20 pm — 19:20
- **d** 11.05 pm — 23:05

3 Measure each line to the nearest mm.

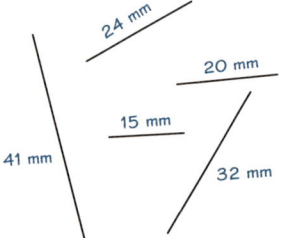

24 mm, 20 mm, 15 mm, 41 mm, 32 mm

4 Label each reading on the scale.

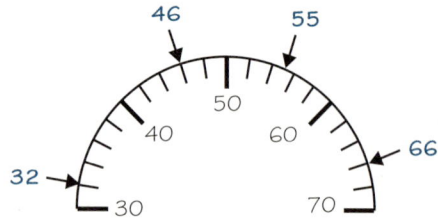

46, 55

Exam practice

1.

The man is average height. The house and the man are drawn to the same scale.

(a) Write down an estimate for the real height of the man in metres. **1.5 m**

(b) Work out an estimate for the real height of the house in metres.

Drawing:
Height of house = 5.5 × height of man
Real life: Height of house = 5.5 × 2
= 11 m

2. This is part of a train timetable from Leeds to Bingley.

Leeds	08:40	09:10	09:33	09:59
Shipley	08:53	09:23	09:48	10:12
Bingley	09:00	09:27	09:52	10:17

(a) Ashley says that the 09 59 train is the quickest. Is she correct? Explain your answer.

No. The 09:10 train takes 17 minutes which is 1 minute quicker.

Deepak lives in Leeds and works in Bingley. It takes him 18 minutes to walk to Leeds train station and 5 minutes to buy a ticket.

(b) What is the latest he can leave home if he wants to catch the 09:10 train?

18 + 5 = 23
09:10 − 23 = 08:47

08:47

Workout 17 answers

18 Compound measures

Reps

1 Write 'speed', 'density' or 'pressure' after each unit.

- **a** km/h — speed
- **b** N/cm² — pressure
- **c** g/cm³ — density
- **d** m/s — speed

2 A cyclist travels 30 km. Work out her average speed if she takes

- **a** 6 hours — 5 km/h
- **b** 2.5 hours — 12 km/h
- **c** 90 minutes — 20 km/h
- **d** $1\frac{1}{4}$ hours — 24 km/h

3 Complete the missing values in the table.

	Mass (g)	Volume (cm³)	Density (g/cm³)
a	100	8	12.5
b	660	300	2.2
c	400	250	1.6

4 Convert

- **a** 0.8 m² into cm² — 8000 cm²
- **b** 300 mm³ into cm³ — 0.3 cm³
- **c** 0.025 km² into m² — 25 000 m²
- **d** 0.004 m³ into cm³ — 4000 cm³

Exam practice

1. An iron block has a mass of 280 g. The density of iron is 7.9 g/cm³. Work out the volume of the block. Give your answer correct to 1 decimal place.

$V = \dfrac{M}{D} = \dfrac{280}{7.9} = 35.4430\ldots$

<u>35.4</u> cm³

2. Two friends drove at constant speeds on the M8 from Glasgow to Edinburgh. Hamid took $1\frac{1}{2}$ hours to complete the 75 km journey. Chloe started her journey 15 minutes after Hamid, and caught up with him 45 minutes later. Work out Chloe's speed, correct to 1 decimal place.

Hamid's speed $= \dfrac{D}{T} = \dfrac{75}{1.5} = 50$ km/h

After 1 hour he had travelled 50 km

Chloe's speed $= \dfrac{D}{T} = \dfrac{50}{0.75}$
$= 66.66\ldots$

<u>66.7</u> km/h

Answers

19 All the angles

Reps

1 Write in the missing angles on this diagram.

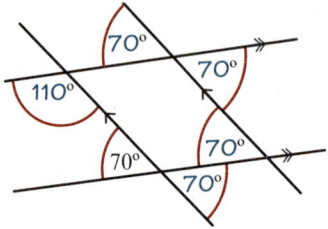

2 Write in the missing angles on this diagram.

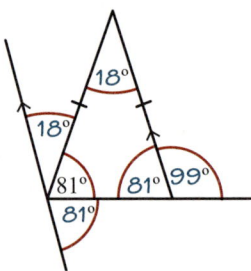

3 Complete the missing values in the table showing angles in regular polygons.

Number of sides	Interior angle	Exterior angle
4	90°	90°
8	135°	45°
20	162°	18°

Exam practice

1. In the diagram, *ABFE* is a parallelogram. *BCD* and *DEF* are straight lines.

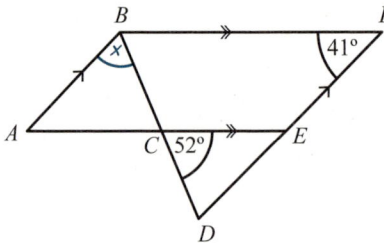

Angle *DCE* = 52° and angle *BFE* = 41°.
Show that angle *ABC* = 87°.

Angle ACB = 52° Reason: Vertically opposite angles are equal
Angle BAC = 41° Reason: Opposite angles in a parallelogram are equal
So 52° + 41° + x = 180°
Reason: Angles in a triangle add up to 180°
x = 180 − 93 = 87°

2. The diagram shows a hexagon. The two angles marked x are equal in size. Work out the value of x.

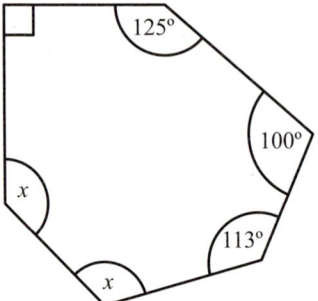

Sum of interior angles =
180° × (6 − 2) = 180° × 4
 = 720°
125 + 100 + 113 + 90 = 428
720 − 428 = 292
292 ÷ 2 = 146

x = 146°

Workout 19 answers

20 Perimeter and area

Reps

Fill in the missing values.

a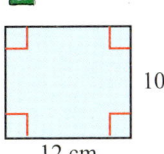

Area = **120** cm²
Perimeter = **44** cm

b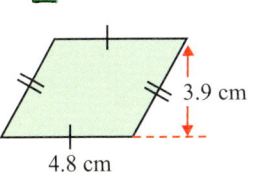

Area = **18.72** cm²
Perimeter = **10.2** cm

c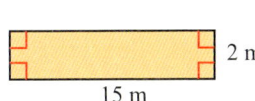

Area = **30** m²
Perimeter = **34** m

d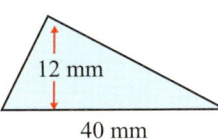

Area = **240** mm²

e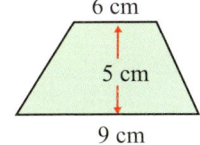

Area = **37.5** cm²

f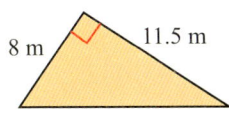

Area = **46** m²

Exam practice

1. This triangle and rectangle have the same area.

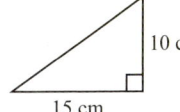 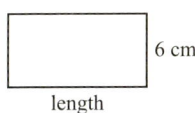

Work out the length of the rectangle.

Area of triangle = $\frac{1}{2} \times b \times h$
$= \frac{1}{2} \times 15 \times 10$
$= 75$ cm²
Area of rectangle = length × 6
75 = length × 6
length = $75 \div 6$
$= 12.5$ cm

2. Six identical rectangles are used to make this larger rectangle.

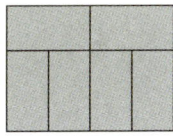

The perimeter of the larger rectangle is 63 cm.

Work out the area of **one** of the smaller rectangles.

Width = x so length = $2x$
Perimeter = $2x + 2x + 2x + 2x + 6x$
$= 14x$
$14x = 63$
$x = 4.5$
Area = $2x \times x = 2 \times 4.5 \times 4.5$
$= 40.5$

40.5 cm²

Answers

21 3-D shapes

Reps

Fill in the missing values.

a
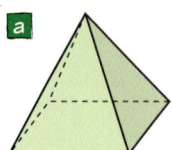
Faces = 5
Edges = 8
Vertices = 5

b
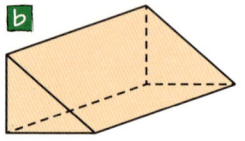
Faces = 5
Edges = 9
Vertices = 6

c
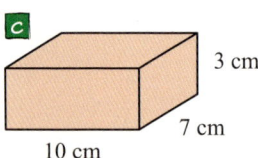
Volume = 210 cm³
Surface area = 242 cm²

d
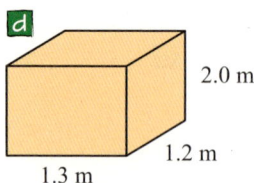
Volume = 4.32 m³
Surface area = 16.32 m²

Exam practice

1. The total surface area of a cube is 150 cm². Work out the volume of the cube.

Area of each face = 150 ÷ 6
= 25 cm²
Length of each side = √25
= 5 cm
Volume = 5 × 5 × 5
= 125

125 cm³

2. Here is a prism. The cross-section of the prism is in the shape of a trapezium.

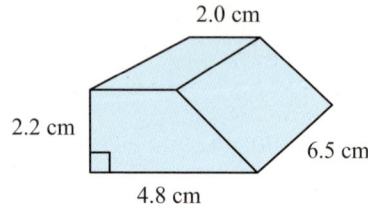

Work out the volume of the prism.

Area = ½ × (a + b) × h
= ½ × (4.8 + 2.0) × 2.2
= ½ × 6.8 × 2.2
= 7.48 cm²
Volume = 7.48 × 6.5 = 48.62

48.62 cm³

22 Circles and cylinders

Reps

1 Work out the area and circumference of each circle to the nearest whole number.

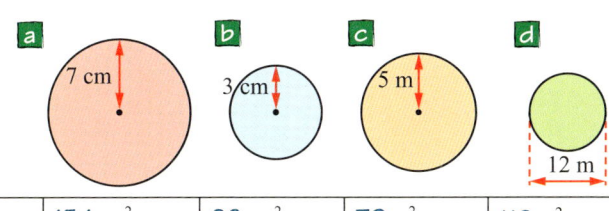

	a	b	c	d
Area	154 cm²	28 cm²	79 m²	113 m²
Circumference	44 cm	19 cm	31 m	38 m

2 Work out the volume of each cylinder to the nearest whole number.

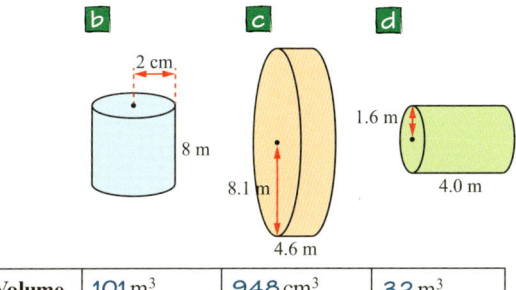

	b	c	d
Volume	101 m³	948 cm³	32 m³

Exam practice

1. The diagram shows a semicircle with a diameter of 24 cm.
   (a) Work out the area of the semicircle.

   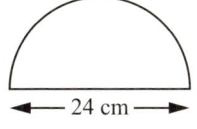

   Radius = 24 ÷ 2 = 12 cm
   Area of whole circle = πr^2 = π × 12²
   = 452.389 cm²
   Area of semicircle = 452.389 ÷ 2
   = 226.2 cm²

   (b) Work out the perimeter of the semicircle.
   Circumference = $2\pi r$
   = 2 × π × 12
   = 75.398
   Perimeter = 24 + $\frac{1}{2}$ × 75.398 = 61.7
   61.7 cm

2. The diagram shows part of a roundabout. The shaded area needs to be planted with grass seed. Each packet of seed covers 12 m². How many packets of grass seed will be needed? You must show your working.

   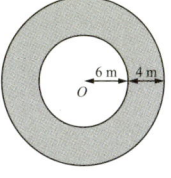

   π × 10² − π × 6² = 201.06...
   201.06... ÷ 12 = 16.75...
   17 packets will be needed.

Answers

23 Transformations

Reps

1 On the grid, transform **T** by

A: translation by vector $\begin{pmatrix} 4 \\ -3 \end{pmatrix}$

B: rotation 90° clockwise about O

C: enlargement centre O with scale factor 2

D: translation by vector $\begin{pmatrix} 0 \\ 5 \end{pmatrix}$

E: reflection in line $x = 4$

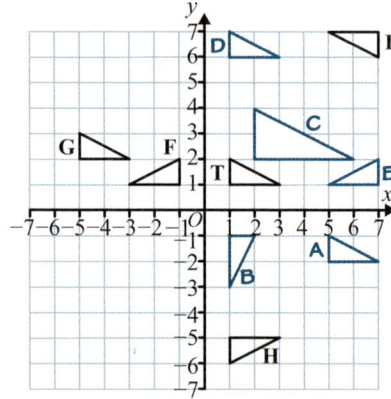

2 Describe the transformation from **T** to

G: translation by vector $\begin{pmatrix} -6 \\ 1 \end{pmatrix}$

H: reflection in line $y = -2$

I: rotation 180° about (4, 4)

Exam practice

1.

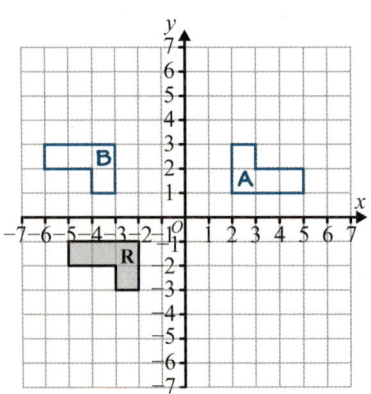

(a) Rotate shape **R** 180° about the origin. Label the new shape **A**.
(b) Translate shape **R** by the vector $\begin{pmatrix} -1 \\ 4 \end{pmatrix}$. Label the new shape **B**.

2.

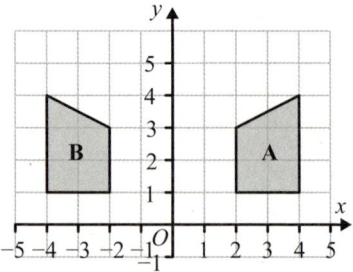

Describe fully the single transformation that maps shape **A** onto shape **B**.

Reflection in the y-axis

Workout 23 answers

24 Pythagoras and trigonometry

Reps

1 Find the lengths of the missing sides in these triangles to 1 decimal place.

a 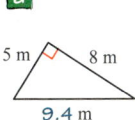   **b** 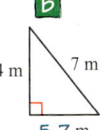   **c**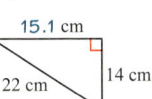

2 Find the sizes of the missing angles to the nearest degree.

a 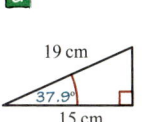   **b** 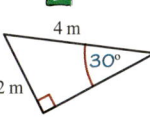   **c**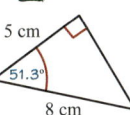

3 Find the lengths of the missing sides in these triangles to 1 decimal place.

a 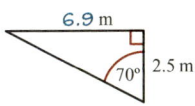   **b** 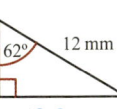   **c**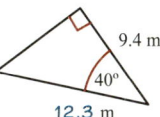

Exam practice

1. ABC is a right-angled triangle.

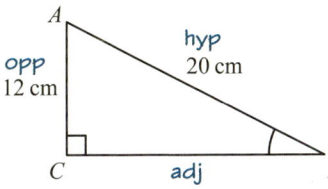

Work out the size of angle ABC. Give your answer to 1 decimal place.

$\sin x = \dfrac{\text{opp}}{\text{hyp}}$

$= \dfrac{12}{20} = 0.6$

$x = \sin^{-1} 0.6 = 36.9°$

36.9°

2. Here is a triangular prism.

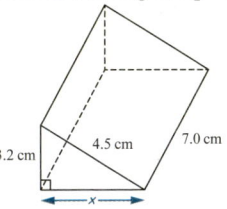

Work out the volume of the prism. Give your answer correct to 1 decimal place.

$x^2 + 3.2^2 = 4.5^2$

$x^2 = 20.25 - 10.24$

$\quad\;\; = 10.01$

$x = 3.163... \text{ cm}$

Area of cross-section $= \dfrac{1}{2} \times b \times h$

$= \dfrac{1}{2} \times 3.163... \times 3.2$

$= 5.062...\text{ cm}^2$

Volume of prism $= 5.062... \times 7.0$

$= 35.4 \text{ cm}^3$

25 Bearings and constructions

Reps

1 Construct an equilateral triangle with sides of length 4cm. Label a 60° angle on your triangle.

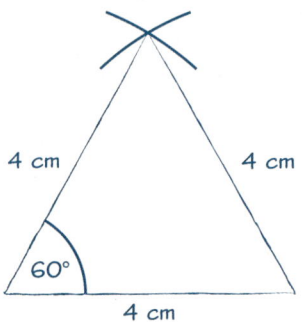

2 Bisect this angle using a ruler and compasses.

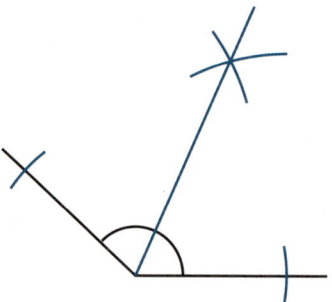

Exam practice

1. Using a ruler and a pair of compasses, accurately construct a perpendicular to this straight line that passes through the point *P*.

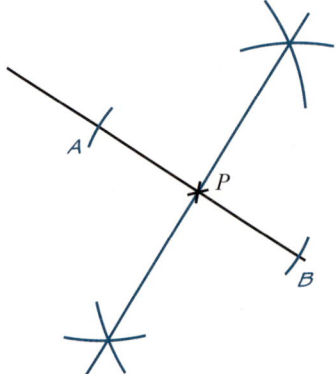

2. The diagram shows two villages on a map.

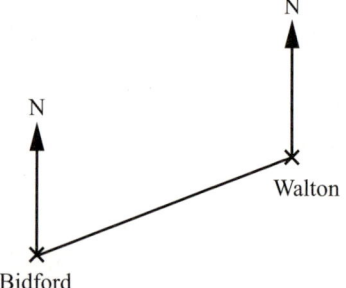

(a) Find the bearing of Bidford from Walton.

261°

(b) Martin writes down the bearing of Walton from Bidford as 81°. What mistake has Martin made?

He should have written his answer with three figures as 081°.

26 Similar and congruent

Reps

1 Find the missing lengths in each pair of similar shapes.

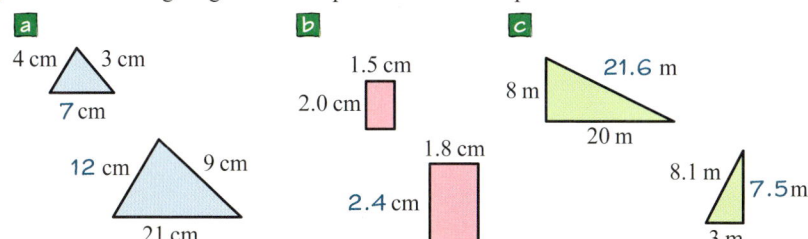

2 Write down the condition that shows that each pair of triangles is congruent.

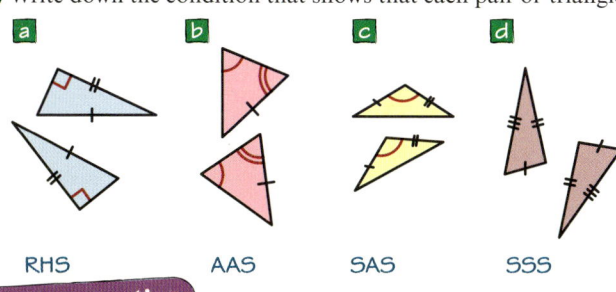

RHS   AAS   SAS   SSS

Exam practice

1. Triangle ABC is mathematically similar to triangle PQR.

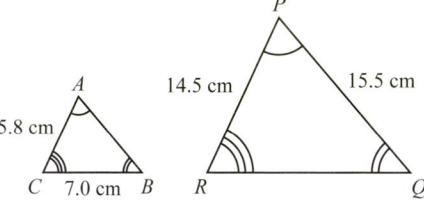

(a) Work out the length of QR.

$\frac{14.4}{5.8} = 2.5$

$7.0 \times 2.5 = 17.5$

17.5 cm

(b) Work out the length of AB.

$15.5 \div 2.5 = 6.2$

6.2 cm

2. Show that these two triangles are mathematically similar.

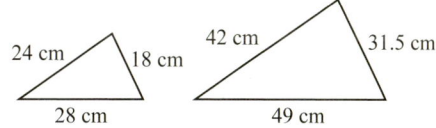

$\frac{31.5}{18} = 1.75$

$\frac{42}{24} = 1.75$

$\frac{49}{28} = 1.75$

Corresponding sides are in the same ratio so the two triangles are mathematically similar.

Workout 26 answers

27 Graphs and charts

Reps

1 The scatter graph shows the hourly cost of parking at 11 different car parks, and their distance from the town centre.

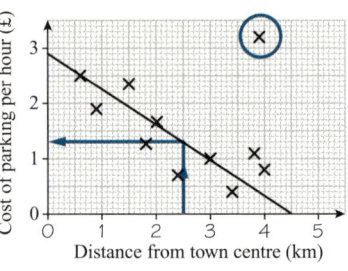

a One point is an outlier. Circle this point.

b Write down the type of correlation.

Negative

2 Use the line of best fit to estimate the hourly cost of parking at a car park that is

a 1.2 km from the town centre £2.10

b 4 km from the town centre £0.30

Exam practice

1. This pictogram shows the number of cars sold last month by two different salespeople.

Emma	◐◐◐◐◐◑
Takeshi	◐◐◐◐

Key: ◐ represents **3 cars**

Write down one thing that is wrong with this pictogram.

Half of the key would represent 1.5 cars and it is not possible to sell half a car.

2. A group of people were asked what their favourite food to buy at the cinema was. The table shows their answers.

Food	Frequency	Angle
Sweets	9	9 × 10° = 90°
Popcorn	20	20 × 10° = 200°
Nachos	7	7 × 10° = 70°

Draw an accurate pie chart for this information.

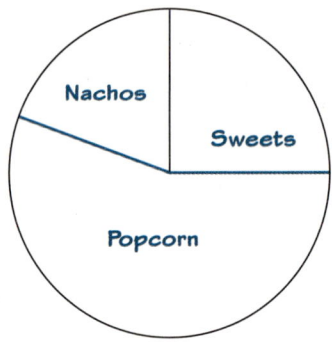

Total frequency = 9 + 20 + 7 = 36
Angle for 1 person = 360° ÷ 36 = 10°

Workout 27 answers

28 Averages and range

Reps

1 For each set of data values, find the mean, the median and the range.

a) 1.4 2.0 2.1 3.5   Mean = 2.25   Median = 2.05   Range = 2.1
b) 2 2 3 4 8 8   Mean = 4.5   Median = 3.5   Range = 6
c) 2 7 8 5 5   Mean = 5.4   Median = 5   Range = 6
d) 10 15 22 13   Mean = 15   Median = 14   Range = 12

2 This frequency table shows the heights of some plants. Complete the table and find the mean and the class interval that contains the median.

Height, h (cm)	Frequency, f	Midpoint, x	$f \times x$
$0 \leq h < 10$	36	5	36 × 5 = 180
$10 \leq h < 20$	40	15	40 × 15 = 600
$20 \leq h < 30$	24	25	24 × 25 = 600
Totals	100		1380

Mean = 13.8 cm   Class interval containing median = $10 \leq h < 20$

Exam practice

1. The frequency table shows the number of trips abroad taken by each member of a class in the last year.

Number of trips	Frequency	$f \times x$
0	8	8 × 0 = 0
1	10	10 × 1 = 10
2	7	7 × 2 = 14
3	5	5 × 3 = 15
4	1	1 × 4 = 4
Total	31	43

(a) Work out the mean number of trips.

Mean = $\frac{43}{31}$ = 1.387...   1.4

(b) What was the median number of trips?

16th value is in class interval 1 trip   1

2. The mean of the following five numbers is 12.6

18   7 x 16 x

Find the value of x.

$18 + 7 + x + 16 + x = 12.6 \times 5$
$2x + 41 = 63$
$2x = 63 - 41$
$2x = 22$
$x = \frac{22}{2}$
$x = 11$

$x = 11$

29 Probability

Reps

1 Draw a line to match each word to the correct place on the probability scale.

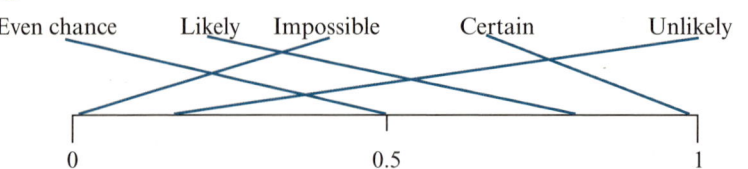

2 A fair six-sided dice is thrown. Find the probability of getting

a. an even number — $\frac{3}{6}$ or $\frac{1}{2}$
b. a square number — $\frac{2}{6}$ or $\frac{1}{3}$
c. a number less than 6 — $\frac{5}{6}$
d. a number more than 7 — 0

3 A fair coin is tossed three times. Find the probability of getting

a. three tails — $\frac{1}{8}$
b. tails on the last toss — $\frac{1}{2}$
c. heads on the first toss — $\frac{1}{2}$
d. tails on the first two tosses — $\frac{1}{4}$

Exam practice

1. A bag contains 10 counters. They are
3 black squares   2 white squares
1 black circle   4 white circles
Soujit takes a counter at random.

(a) Show that the probability of taking a white counter is $\frac{3}{5}$.

$2 + 4 = 6$

$P(\text{white}) = \frac{6}{10} = \frac{3}{5}$

Soujit returns the counter to the bag and picks another one at random. He does this experiment 50 times.

(b) Work out an estimate for the number of times he picks a white counter.

$\frac{3}{5} \times 50 = 30$

.30.

2. A spinner can land on red or green or blue. The table shows the probabilities of landing on red or green.

Colour	Red	Green	Blue
Probability	0.2	0.5	

The spinner is spun once.

(a) Work out the probability of landing on blue.

$1 - 0.2 - 0.5 = 0.3$

0.3

The spinner is spun twice.

(b) Work out the probability of landing on the same colour twice.

$P(\text{red, red}) = 0.2 \times 0.2 = 0.04$
$P(\text{green, green}) = 0.5 \times 0.5 = 0.25$
$P(\text{blue, blue}) = 0.3 \times 0.3 = 0.09$
$P(\text{same colour}) = 0.04 + 0.25 + 0.09$
$= 0.38$

Workout 29 answers

30 Venn diagrams

Reps

Shade the events shown, and write down the probability of each event.

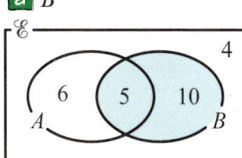

P(B) = $\frac{15}{25}$

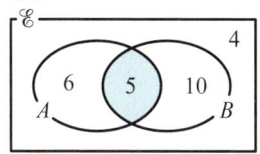

P(A ∩ B) = $\frac{5}{25}$

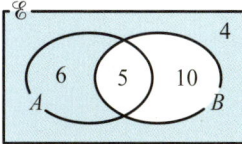

P(Not B) = $\frac{10}{25}$

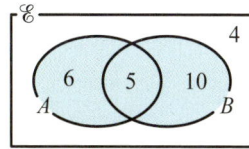

P(A ∪ B) = $\frac{21}{25}$

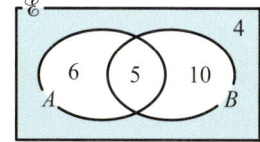

P(Neither A nor B) = $\frac{4}{25}$

Exam practice

1. There are 650 students at a college.
   429 of them have passed their driving test.
   185 males have passed their driving test.
   290 students are male.
   Use this information to complete the frequency tree.

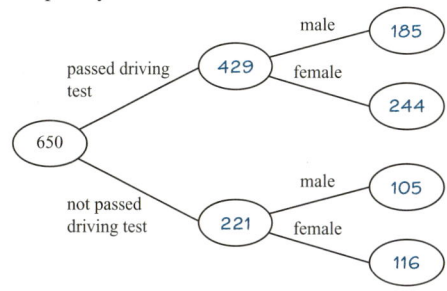

2. $\mathcal{E}$ = {prime numbers less than 30}
   A = {2, 7, 11, 23}
   B = {3, 5, 7}

   (a) Complete the Venn diagram to show this information.

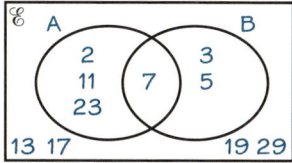

A number is chosen at random from the universal set $\mathcal{E}$.

(b) What is the probability that it is in the set A ∪ B?

$\frac{6}{10}$

Published by Pearson Education Limited, 80 Strand, London, WC2R 0RL.

www.pearsonschoolsandfecolleges.co.uk

Copies of official specifications for all Pearson qualifications may be found on the website: qualifications.pearson.com

Text © Harry Smith and Pearson Education Ltd 2019
Original illustrations © Pearson Education Ltd 2019
Typeset by Newgen KnowledgeWorks (P) Ltd, Chennai, India
Produced by Newgen Publishing UK, Stroud
Cover illustration by Miriam Sturdee

The right of Harry Smith to be identified as author of this work has been asserted by him in accordance with the Copyright, Designs and Patents Act 1988.

First published 2019

22 21 20 19
10 9 8 7 6 5 4 3 2 1

British Library Cataloguing in Publication Data

A catalogue record for this book is available from the British Library

ISBN 978 1 292 24690 1

Copyright notice

All rights reserved. No part of this publication may be reproduced in any form or by any means (including photocopying or storing it in any medium by electronic means and whether or not transiently or incidentally to some other use of this publication) without the written permission of the copyright owner, except in accordance with the provisions of the Copyright, Designs and Patents Act 1988 or under the terms of a licence issued by the Copyright Licensing Agency, Barnard's Inn, 86 Fetter Lane, London EC4A 1EN (www.cla.co.uk). Applications for the copyright owner's written permission should be addressed to the publisher.

Printed in Italy by L.E.G.O. S.p.A.

Notes from the publisher

1. While the publishers have made every attempt to ensure that advice on the qualification and its assessment is accurate, the official specification and associated assessment guidance materials are the only authoritative source of information and should always be referred to for definitive guidance.

   Pearson examiners have not contributed to any sections in this resource relevant to examination papers for which they have responsibility.

2. Pearson has robust editorial processes, including answer and fact checks, to ensure the accuracy of the content in this publication, and every effort is made to ensure this publication is free of errors. We are, however, only human, and occasionally errors do occur. Pearson is not liable for any misunderstandings that arise as a result of errors in this publication, but it is our priority to ensure that the content is accurate. If you spot an error, please do contact us at resourcescorrections@pearson.com so we can make sure it is corrected.